A Whirlwind's Breath

A Memoir of Faith and Healing at Indiana's Riley Hospital

Judy Chatham

Author's Tranquility Press
ATLANTA, GEORGIA

Judy Chatham / Author's Tranquility Press
3900 N Commerce Dr. Suite 300 #1255
Atlanta, GA 30344
www.authorstranquilitypress.com

Ordering Information:
Quantity sales. Special discounts are available on quantity purchases by corporations, associations, and others. For details, contact the "Special Sales Department" at the address above.

A Whirlwind's Breath / Judy Chatham
Hardback: 978-1-964810-79-9
Paperback: 978-1-964810-80-5
eBook: 978-1-964810-81-2

For my Sons—

Stephen and Brian Chatham

And

For all who have heard the words,

"There's a suspicious looking spot here."
"This may be an abnormality.
This is cancer."

Stephen (1) and Brian Jay

My layperson's perception of medical procedures and the doctor's scientific descriptions could differ. Therefore, I should not be quoted as an expert.

Names of medical personnel have been changed, except that of Dr. Arthur Provisor.

PROLOGUE

My life began in rural Southern Indiana, where people do not have to stage a fall festival or invent a rural village scene. We lived that life which included cutting up squash for pies, planting dahlias along the garden's edge, and making faces after devouring puckery persimmons.

A few in our neighborhood had natural springs from which piped, cool water ran continuously into their kitchen's artisan box. The older children played in haylofts, helped pick blackberries, explored a cave which we had named "bear cave," and made gathered- waist dresses for the 4-H county fair. While today people pay admission to see Hoosier-made Dutch Boy or flower garden quilts, for me, there was no admission fee, for quilt frames were put up in a well-lighted room in our home each winter of my childhood.

The wholesomeness of my early life has much to do with the story I am about to tell, for when I faced the possibility of our two sons' deaths from fatal illnesses, that secure upbringing proved to be both a hindrance and a blessing. On the one hand, my sheltered life was underscored by a firm foundation from which I would "work out my faith in fear and trembling."

Even the title of this book comes form early years when I played "Faith is the Victory" on our upright piano. Such diligent deciphering between sharps and flats caused me to repeat every word of every hymn. It was in verse two, a verse of praise to the saints of old that I found my lines ...

By faith, they like a whirlwind's breath,
Swept o'er every field,
The faith by which they conquered death
Will be our conquering shield.

It Is the hope that others in the midst of a serious illness will benefit from our experience that prompts me to share our story here. May it bring blessing.

Judith McCart Chatham
July 2024

A Whirlwind's Breath

Daily I walked up and down the halls of the teen unit and frowned at the grinning jack-o-lanterns and sparsely clothed skeletons hanging on each door. Yes, it was Halloween, and teens do like Halloween. However, I now saw this holiday I had always enjoyed as a major part of a cruel joke. Undoubtedly, the well-meaning volunteers did not have a child with acute cancer, for they would have viewed those skeletons as hideous, not merely as an amusement. True to its Celtic tradition, Halloween had become the beginning of the season of cold and darkness, and certainly it was that to me.

As I looked around at this grotesque décor, I reviewed the details of what seemed to be a grim joke on us: God had known all along. He had known when little Stephen first began to walk and talk. God had known when Stephen first played Little League basketball. "Enjoy it now, son, for soon you will die." God had known long before that bone scan taken on the day of diagnosis. He knew, and He had chosen to do nothing to protect our child.

***

Cancer plays a waiting and listening game with those who suffer from its invasion, whether that person be the one who is ill or the one who is the caretaker. Our waiting and listening began on a Sunday evening after our fourteen-year-old son Stephen, with his eighth-grade school friend Jeff, had returned from a school vacation trip to Jamestown, Virginia, and to Washington, D.C.

"When I got out of the car at the Lincoln Memorial, I could hardly walk," he said. "I was so weak. Then when I tried to climb those steps of the Memorial, I couldn't keep up with Jeff. I thought I was going to have to sit down and rest before I got to the top."

His cracked, bleached-out lips and his paper-white skin helped me to formulate my own diagnosis. Having tallied the symptoms, I looked at him, really looked at him with a mother's searching eye. Few answers came through my fingertips as I ran them down both sides of his neck. Surely he had strep infection. From his earlobes to his shoulders, down both sides, the lymph glands were swollen so taut he winced each time he turned his head. Yet he claimed his throat was not sore.

Four hours after my own diagnosis, we learned the doctor's preliminary diagnosis. Barry, my husband, called from the hospital's emergency room, to report that the Sunday evening doctor "wanted him to go by ambulance to Riley Hospital for Children. I told them I would drive him myself. They claim there's something wrong with his blood."

Because our other son was asleep, we decided I should stay home with him. Fully dressed, in case I needed to leave in a hurry, I went to bed leaving the lights on in every room of the house except in twelve-year-old Brian's room. The light somehow made me feel safer; it was as though the darkness were an additional threat. My eyes never closed. Even though I must have had five heavy blankets over me, I shivered. My teeth chattered; my head ached. Over and over I told myself "everything will be OK." Over and over I named diseases "that wouldn't be so bad," never daring to name the something that could be fatal.

Riley Hospital for Children admitted Stephen, and hematologists quickly moved into a battery of testing that lasted for three more hours. Sometime between 2:00 and 3:00 AM, Barry, confused and exhausted, but determined to stay at the hospital, called to say, "The doctors and several interns came into the room and announced, 'Everyone's tired. All of us need some sleep. Dr. Smith will see you and your wife in his office at 11:00 AM tomorrow.'"

The next morning, as I walked into the hospital, I noticed the Raggedy Ann and Andy dolls perched inside the curves of the letters RILEY HOSPITAL FOR CHILDREN. The rag dolls whimsically seated inside the letters took the zing out of the emergency-like electricity of the hallways. For sure, patients in this hospital were very ill. No visitor to any floor would say, "I wonder why this girl is a patient here? She looks so well."

I had seen children with the usual childhood diseases—chicken pox and measles. I had touched children with a body temperature of 104°, but I had never seen a child who was ill unto death. Thinking I was on the teen-unit floor, I walked along the hallway searching for my own son's room. Little red wagons carried children whose IV poles were held high above the wagons. Mothers chatted as they pulled their children along.

Then I met a nurse who carried a toddler—I can see his crew cut yet. He was draped over her shoulder, his little head falling to one side like the blossom of a flower whose stem had broken. Soon I realized his little neck was so weak he could no longer hold up his head. Then I saw his eyes—those knowing eyes that had seen the same things that the elderly see near the end of their lives.

Hurrying to run away from this new world that would soon be my home in the months ahead, I took the elevator to the unit. On the elevator I stood beside a woman who had just left the toddler floor. She lamented to the friend beside her, "I was on the phone in the kitchen, and she just tumbled into the mop bucket—head first. It couldn't have been more than seconds when I pulled her out."

Trying not to look at her, I thought, "How did I become 'lumped in' with this irresponsible person? I'm a good mother. I've taken care of my children."

Down the hallway in the teen unit, I slowly passed the rooms where young people lay, hooked to IV solutions, nutrients, medication, oxygen or blood transfusions—with monitors clicking away the time. Their parents "held up the walls" in the hallway or sprawled in the very small 8'x10' waiting room, having what appeared to be another med center specialty: a chocolate chip cookie, or a Hostess Ding Dong or Twinkie. I remember thinking how they looked too much at home. How long had these people been here? I noted many were overweight and unfit, heavy shells trying to move through another day.

Once inside Stephen's room, my fears evaporated. "Last night's vigil was totally unnecessary," I told myself. Reasoning that only a mother knows when her child is ill, I relaxed. Even my husband Barry's red eyes and swollen face did not startle me. Obviously, he too had been taken in by this fiasco. Selectively overlooking the blood transfusion-in-progress, I announced that Stephen's healthy complexion had returned. All he needed was a little rest. He grinned in agreement. Then with total confidence, I walked down the corridor ahead of Barry, who by now had been reduced to a shaky, teary-eyed dad. On we walked, en route to the doctor's consultation room for the three of us to "talk." On this business-as-usual

Monday morning in late October, at exactly 11:30 AM, Dr. Smith faced us, and maintaining perfect eye contact said, "Stephen has leukemia."

After a few moments of total silence, he told us that in 1978 approximately one in 10,000 children in Indiana had childhood cancer. Immediately, I remembered the admonition I had heard all of my life: **Do not gamble.** So what was this but gambling? Our odds were one in 10,000 and in that moment we had just lost a child. Life had suddenly become a game, and "chance" would undoubtedly become a prominent word in our vocabulary.

Next Dr. Smith began to review what we could expect. First, he told us that acute lymphocytic leukemia is the childhood version of the disease in which the white cells devour the red cells at a rapidly moving rate. He explained that the severe leg pain Stephen had experienced was the result of this abnormal packing of a large number of white blood cells into the bone marrow of his legs. The chalk-white face, the colorless lips were manifestations of the drain of red blood cells in his body.

Dr. Smith went on to explain what we could expect in the weeks ahead. First Stephen might develop diabetes. Then in two weeks after chemotherapy began, his hair would begin to fall out. Of course, with chemotherapy, infection was the great concern since the body's defenses might become depleted. Often an unusual brand of pneumonia would develop, one that antibiotics could not touch. The body's ravaged defenses would simply have to take over at that point—scenarios of the future popped like proverbial flashbulbs in my mind.

"I'll excuse myself for a few minutes, then I'll return to accompany you when I relay the diagnosis to Stephen," Dr. Smith said as though he were really asking a question rather than informing us of the next step.

How odd that I recall how he left the room. He walked through the doorway like one does when walking out of a prayer meeting. The door closed one inch at a time, very carefully, very quietly.

While I don't recall the exact conversation between Barry and me, I do recall the angry tone. I also recall that we referred to God immediately. The essence of our conversation went something like this: "How could God allow this terrible thing to happen in a family where every member is in church each Sunday and where both mother and father work very hard in many areas of church activities?"

I also remember how I mentally began to dredge up knowledge of leukemia, what I had learned while I worked in the lab at a county hospital between my years in college. Over a decade later I could still see the purple-stained slide of a blood smear which revealed the blasts of leukemia. Even I, the English major, could see the abnormal clumping on that slide. Based on that recollection, I knew there was no need to seek a second opinion on this diagnosis of Stephen's condition. Valuable time would be lost if we delayed treatment. Then, as an added twist to that county hospital recollection, I felt ungrateful for the early insight. I saw that training as a foreshadowing into my life story. Did He simply spend His days amusing Himself with such trickery?

It was with that not-so-thinly-veiled accusation that I went to Stephen's bedside to comfort him as he, too, learned the diagnosis. With Barry standing beside his bed and me sitting on the bed beside him, a doctor began to speak. Two hematologists surrounded by six to eight white-coated interns delivered the news.

One doctor said, "Steve, you have acute lymphocytic leukemia. Do you know what leukemia is?" Stephen told him he had read about it in science class.

"Do you have any questions?" the doctor asked him.

"No." Stephen quietly answered him.

With that "No" the interns began writing on their clipboards. No doubt, this had been an observation for a class assignment. The interns needed to write a paper on a child's reaction to the diagnosis of cancer. All three of us felt cornered, trapped into some kind of class experiment. The doctors left the room, and Stephen began to yawn. In the months ahead, I would learn that this yawn was his reaction to disturbing news.

Our little conservative politician, alone in his thoughts. Our Stephen—only yesterday I had seen his six-year-old body bobbing up the broken sidewalk from the fire station near our house. Talking to himself, he was a big boy in a world of his own. A can-do person, now he was that little boy again. Dark brown hair, average height and weight, looking like childhood pictures of hundreds of little boys the world over, yet our handsome little man was desperately ill.

Once at home, I pulled out his baby book which recorded all of his immunization records. Doctors needed those dates and any other information about childhood illnesses, especially the chickenpox virus, which is far from compatible with leukemia and chemotherapy. While rustling through the baby book, I came upon the baby footprint, the lock of hair, the date when Stephen took his first steps, and pictures of him with his little brother on the first day of school.

Always the one with the positive attitude, Stephen would say, "I can do it." He loved being with a group of neighborhood kids, loved to be one of the pack, a real team player. Like most teenagers, he never wanted to be different or be on the outside looking in. He always wanted to be the participant and not the spectator. Once when I suggested we drive by a newly constructed ski resort, he asked, "Why? Why would we want to drive by and see a ski resort?" If we had no skis with us, then why simply drive by and look? If you couldn't get in there and ski—forget it!

Now the long days in bed separated him from the group and from participating. He was different, and, for him, this was the worst. Also, he was fourteen and adolescence was upon him; yet at home, when he would lie in bed with high body temperature and nausea, we, the protective parents, were undoubtedly seeing him as a little boy again. On those occasions, when he was feeling well enough to care, these conflicting images no doubt grated on him.

One night, when his body felt so warm we wondered why his blood didn't boil, I washed his face and arms with a cool cloth. As I tried to distract him from his thoughts of the illness, he began to tell me when he was well he would soon be going to Jackson Hole, Wyoming. He *would* ski down the highest slope.

Some years after Stephen's diagnosis, I wrote a poem about waiting and listening. That's what a cancer patient and the loved one does . . . waits and listens for test results, for changes, for good news. Our son was an extension of us, and, therefore, WE suffered from leukemia. If he died, each of us died. Not knowing for sure what he was feeling, I knew we were feeling like our world was suddenly spinning out of control. Over and over we discussed how we were on a merry-go-round that was moving too fast. We were hurled from one development to another, then soothed just enough to prepare for the next onslaught. Through it all, I waited and listened. Maybe there would be a word of hope, a word of encouragement.

A WHIRLWIND'S BREATH

Karen and I saw it coming
Down by the garden
Whirling among the orchard's
Pear trees.
At first it spun low to the ground,
But by the time it reached
The big oak that Grandma
Had grazed on her first and final
Driving lesson,
It picked up enough dust
To spread wide and accelerate
Full speed ahead.

From our perch on the porch swing,
We watched intently as it followed
The road, passing the apple trees
And heading straight for the lilac bush
A top spinning with more determination
Than I had ever witnessed,
It wheeled around the lilac
And the top of the well, skipped the coal pile,
Ducked under the lowest limbs
Of the tulip tree,
And executed a flourish,
As if to wave to the viewers
On the porch swing.
Then it whistled by the hop vine
That Grandma had tied with twine
To the corner post of the porch,
And smooth as my daddy's whistle,
It spun completely out of sight.

Amazed, we children sat quietly
For a few moments,
Reviewing what we had seen
And listening for a crash

Somewhere in the backyard,
As the whirlwind would surely
Collide with something in its path.
Not moving a muscle,
We waited,
     We listened.

Once we had felt the
Warmth of the whirlwind's breath,
We never forgot how powerfully
That swish sailed by.

Today—
Decades late,
We wait,
     We listen.

Judith McCart Chatham
Fall 1978

Two weeks of daily spinal taps, bone marrows, blood transfusions, blood draws, and chemotherapy adjustments in Steve's treatment, and our once normal daily routine was only a memory. Along about this time I recalled the words on a plaque I had once valued during the time of mourning my father's death six years earlier:

Normal day, let me be aware of the treasure
you are. Let me learn from you, love you,
savor you, bless you, before you depart. Let
me not pass you by in quest of some rare and
perfect tomorrow. Let me hold you while I may,
for it will not always be so. One day I will dig
my fingers into the earth, or bury my face in the pillow,
or stretch myself taut, or raise my hands to the sky,
and want more than all the world your return.
—Abbey Press of St. Meinrad, Indiana

Now, I really understood what that verse meant. These days, all anyone in the teen unit heard was related to the word—normal. These children, who could no longer toss the football, engage in idle phone conversation, or blow out candles at the birthday party—all the carefree activities—saw the world passing by. "Please, I just want to be normal, average." I marveled that "normal" and "average" were words whose meaning I had never treasured before.

What was normal for us? Getting up at 6:00 AM to a short order breakfast. Dad ran off to work as director of therapies for nursing homes and hospitals; Brian and Stephen went to the sixth and eighth grades at the middle school; I drove to teach my classes of mythology, literature of the Bible, and English composition at a nearby high school. Then, often, we returned home in the evenings to some kind of ballgame or practice—baseball or basketball. We worked our evening meal around the boys' after-school paper route, games, and our church and school meetings. These were normal times for us.

All of that was part of the white picket fence existence I had dreamed of; however, I did not see these days as treasures as they passed. They included headaches, problems—those porcupines of life to which my friend Susan often referred.

Treasures were vacation days, holidays and weekend days. Now, I longed for a normal day filled with the good and the bad, and if I ever had the good fortune to have one again, I knew I would view it as treasure.

What a difficult time for Steve! What a difficult time for all who loved him! Even with all of the tests, I wondered if the staff of Riley Hospital could heal our son. Yet, in my experience, Riley Hospital for Children had always been the hospital that treated the really serious illnesses of Indiana's children. All county and some city hospitals transferred their children with the illnesses that were not responding to treatment to Riley Hospital for Children as a place that rested under one gigantic guardian angel's wing.

In 1978 we literally took up residence in the children's hospital in the Indiana University Medical Center on Barnhill Drive, Indianapolis. Exactly twenty-two minutes from our house was the hospital with its well-worn, nondescript walls in dire need of new paint. So bleak was the place that I don't even remember if the color was institutional green or light gray. Even the volunteer-sewn curtains and pajamas which had been through frequent washings were faded. "Faded" often fit our moods, yet on many days, we didn't even notice the lack of color so badly needed in this children's hospital soon to be remodeled.

What we did notice were the eyes of the desperately ill. Again, it was the eyes that looked into the depths, the old eyes in the baby faces, in which we saw the questions that rent our hearts, for we were adults who had suffered from nothing more serious than the measles. Likewise, in our own child, it was the eyes that asked some serious questions that no one could answer.

In the late 1970s, Riley Hospital for Children had its share of noise, too, sitting in the heart of an expanding Indiana University Medical Center near West Michigan Avenue, one of Indianapolis busiest streets. That was outside. Inside, little red wagons with high-rise sides transported the children along the corridors and through the steamy tunnels of the Medical Center Complex. For some, the rides were merely recreational, but for others, the rides carried them to the next medical test.

On those days when we went to the Hematology clinic B, the waiting room was packed with children who had wisps of baby-fine hair, new growth on heads that had been bald only days ago. Signs of the work of chemotherapy and radiation were everywhere. "Birthmark purple" marked a radiation therapist's measurement lines on the sides of heads, and no body hair were the most prevalent evidences of the treatment in progress.

The sometimes nerve-wracking clickety-clack pull toys were more than a background hum to the teenage patient and his parents who acutely understood that any checkup could uncover cancer out of remission.

Above all, there were no fish tanks of bubbling water nor piped-in music to sooth the disquieted mind. Instead there was the assault of the television, with mindless scripts of soap operas which all of us watched in order to overlook the ravishes of "our" same cancer in the one seated in the chair beside us. Looking back, one had to wonder if any distraction would have been effective in those Tuesday three-to-four hour waits in clinic B.

It is odd that I do not recall the smells of Riley Hospital in 1978. I do not recall the medicinal aroma that usually wafts out of any medical facility. Yet the hospital clinic was loaded with the components of chemotherapy. Children died at Riley Hospital, yet I do not recall the odor of dying flesh that one is met with upon entering medical facilities where adults are seriously ill. I suppose I didn't smell what I didn't want to smell.

Yet, in 1978, I did notice that Riley Hospital's floors were slick with use. I noticed that walls had been repeatedly knicked with carts that transport the sick. Each gouge of the plaster was like "a red badge of courage" to me. I saw more gray than bright colors, and the nursing staff, while overworked and highly stressed, must have been trained in a convent, for they were caring, patient people. Hospital lights rarely dimmed, and activity, whether it be tests, x-rays or surgery, continued at night as it had in the daytime. Specialists, whom the uninformed might have labeled overpaid and aloof, could be heard in the hallways as clearly at 3:00 AM as at 3:00 PM. It was those people, especially Dr. Arthur Provisor, that we came to appreciate beyond words.

Looking back today, we see days when Stephen must have been dying, but the doctors and nurses never changed the pitch of their voices, as they said, "The body temp is 105°" or "The blood gas indicates we need a tap of the lung to check things out." If the patient's face was the white of plaster, his vision was blurred and his ankles frozen to cause a shuffle, the greeting from the Riley Hospital staff was the same—playful, upbeat, caring, but not condescending—always words that would encourage and spur the teen to push through the next few days because the future could be bright.

Schooling at the hospital was a top priority with the teacher who reported to our room within hours of the first chemotherapy treatment. The program was designed to take the child from where he was in his regular school program, using his own school books and keeping him caught up with homework. As a result, when he returned to school he would be ready to join his classmates with no necessary attention to make-up assignments. The illness was considered temporary no matter how serious it was. The topic of the day was always: What Do You Want To Be When You Grow Up?—or something like that.

A large activity room in the hub of a wheel of patients' rooms was the center of life in the teen unit. Volunteers carted boxes of craft supplies and ingredients for cooking across the Med Center campus in order to provide a few minutes of diversion from thoughts of the scariest of diseases.

The whole hospital displayed gifts and the results of efforts of volunteers from around the state. On the first floor, a doll collection of the wife of 1920s Governor Edward Jackson could be balanced against the efforts of the ladies who carried an ice cream freezer, crushed ice and salt into the hospital to make the home-made ice cream for a party, indeed, all things considered. I could see that Riley Hospital for Children was deservedly held in high regard as the best destination for a seriously ill child.

Indiana's answer to medical care for children, the hospital was founded in 1916 when the Riley Association was formed to perpetuate the memory of the beloved Hoosier poet James Whitcomb Riley. His "The Bear" poem, when recited by memory by an elderly man I knew as Mr. Ralston, had been my favorite when I was a child. However, during these trying times I now meditated upon "The Prayer Perfect" which was painted on the entrance wall:

Dear Lord! Kind Lord!
  Gracious Lord, I pray
Thou wilt look on all I love,
  Tenderly today!
Weed their hearts of weariness,
  Scatter every care
Down a wake of angel-wings
  Winnowing the air.
Bring unto the sorrowing
  All release from pain;
Let the lips of laughter
  Overflow again;
And with all the needy
  O divide, I pray,
This vast treasure of content
  That is mine today!

I continued to teach during the day, drive the thirty miles from school to Indianapolis, stay all night at the hospital, dress in a four foot by four-foot rest room, then return to the high school and teach six classes. In recent years, I have learned that I was teaching what it means to persevere, and the students picked up on the message as it was taught. Oddly, my students, many of who were also in the Fellowship of Christian athletes which I sponsored, said, "you were teaching us something we have needed many times since those often-carefree school days. We learned to be resilient, to persevere, and to not take lightly the upholding of an employment contract. You were present as often as possible."

Teaching school has been both a solace and an albatross around my neck, for only days before the diagnosis of leukemia in my own son, an ominous story unfolded in my second-hour class.

In the fall of 1978, at the meeting for orientation of teachers, I routinely picked up the roll for my five classes. Soon I was given additional information about one of my students. This boy was to be in my sophomore Honors Comp class. Having been diagnosed with leukemia the previous spring, he had responded well to the chemotherapy treatments. The memo said I would note that his hair had fallen out and that his gait was somewhat halting, as though his ankles were no longer flexible. No matter what, I was to treat him like any other student, since that was his request.

One month into the school year, I stood outside my classroom and watched this young man walking down the corridor, alternately shuffling and lifting his feet higher than necessary with each step. I had watched for what seemed like two or three minutes when a fellow teacher joined me and quietly responded by shaking his head as if to say, "That is not good."

Only two weeks later, the young man left for Seattle's Hutchinson Clinic for a bone marrow transplant. Because of his loneliness and because I wanted to do so, I led the class in corresponding with him, for it appeared to me that a dedicated teacher adjusts; she does not overlook outside-of-class concerns. Certainly, I reasoned, an effective teacher would guide this class into the difficult time ahead. Therefore, we started each class period with information about leukemia and an update on this boy's progress. I felt as qualified to talk on the subject as

I did to teach English. Also, I did careful research into the types and treatments of the disease, the updated prognosis for young people with leukemia.

When the research for this boy was as complete as any layperson could possibly compile, I found myself conducting my own primary research on the spot.

I marveled at the irony of this association and the full-blown account of what we could expect as the details of the protocol of Stephen's treatment unfolded, and I soon realized I should not have been surprised. After all, at regular intervals in our lives we had had associations with victims of the disease. In fact, the encounters had been evenly spaced, peppered, as if on purpose, through every three to four years of our lives. As the saying goes, "Old scripts played in my mind."

Our first association with the disease had occurred during our senior year in high school in 1960, when several parents of classmates enjoyed inviting "the group" to their homes for parties. A boy, with whom Barry and I had spent a part of every day, had very youth-oriented, attractive parents. Compared to many of our parents who appeared to have no social life at all, this couple regularly went dancing and enjoyed romantic dinners. Their wholesome, yet youth-oriented lifestyle was ideal. We had one goal: All of us would marry and dance out our days together just as this couple did.

What a crushing blow it was to us when, at the young age of thirty-nine, the husband was diagnosed with leukemia and died only a few weeks later.

Our second encounter with leukemia had come in our junior year in college in 1963 when Elizabeth, with whom we had often double-dated, became seriously ill. A dedicated student of piano, Liz normally climbed the four flights of stairs of the Music Building in order to practice for hours at a time on the grand piano. Suddenly she could no longer climb the stairs. In fact, she actually sat down every few steps to rest. Finally, even after resting, she had to sit down on the steps and literally scoot up the stairs.

When I went to the hospital to see her, I braced myself as I approached her door. Always the gracious one, Liz had anticipated visitor's anxiety, for she had a sign taped to her door: BEWARE:

BUBONIC PLAGUE. All I can remember from that visit was her comment that the opening and closing of her eyes took all of her energy. I recall staring at this normally bubbly person so full of life and ambition for her music and concluded: No matter how diligently she follows these doctors' orders, the disease will win. She lived five years with leukemia before she died.

In 1963 the next encounter with leukemia had occurred during my training days in the hospital lab where I met the little two-year-old Shirley Temple-like girl. It was the stained slide smeared with her blood that taught me how obvious is the abnormality of leukemia. This little toddler died shortly after diagnosis.

Less than three years later when we were fresh out of college with our new teaching jobs, a marriage and a new baby, we met our old enemy again. No sooner had the school year begun than one of the elementary school principals was diagnosed with leukemia. Not long after that shocking news, he died.

Nine years passed. I had almost forgotten about our old stalker. Then the disease resurfaced as I taught a sophomore class of honor students. Yes, as I related earlier, this young man did have leukemia, and yes, he died within the month after Steve's diagnosis. While all of these cases involved different kinds of leukemia, all of them were cancers of the bone marrow, and all of the victims of leukemia in our experience had died from the disease. So what should I think now that my own son was a victim of the stalker?

Day after day, during various hospital stays, I taught classes, and then as I drove away, I cried, sometimes moaning like a wounded animal, driving the thirty miles to the hospital barely able to see where I was going. This selective suffering had become part of a pattern in my daily schedule. Once at the hospital, as if on cue, the weeping stopped. I stepped into the elevator and went directly to our son's room in the "teen-unit." Now, as I look back, I know he was not fooled by my cheerful entrance, but at the time, I was certain we were sparing him from the sorrow we felt.

After the initial diagnosis, Steve was a patient in the hospital for a week. Returning home to what the doctors called a normal schedule, his normally athletic body turned to mush while his face was full-moon-shaped and looked bloated as though it would burst. His protocol included daily tablets of prednisone, 6-M Mercaptopurine (6-MP), a drip procedure of Adriamycin, methotrexate injections into the spine, and Bactrim to help prevent possible pneumonia. The prednisone gave him an unsatisfied appetite that never diminished even in the early hours of the morning when we would hear him warming up chicken soup. "Not to worry," we were told, "for the radiation to his brain and spinal cord, scheduled in three weeks, will reverse the demands of the appetite so much that we will soon long for him to call for a pizza at 2:00 AM once again." Experience proved their predictions to be correct as were their forecasts of a possibly untreatable pneumonia from which he would fight to recover.

The first twenty-two days of December in 1978 were spent beside the hospital bed of a seriously ill son with the dreaded pneumonia. Each day as the late afternoon approached, the "witching hour of rising body temperatures" commenced. Off and on throughout the night, Steve's temperature would rise sharply to 105°, then drop to a welcome 103°, after he had been bathed in cold water. Since I worked during the day, I sat with him each night while my husband worked and prepared paperwork to do during the day shift beside Steve's bed. This schedule suited both our body rhythms and the demands of our jobs. During those twenty-two days while I slept on the cot that we had wedged between his bed and the wall, I lay with one hand on his arm. Even in my dozing, I could feel the temperature rise. By the end of the bout with pneumonia, I could tell the nurse his body temperature with accuracy even before she inserted the thermometer under his tongue. Finally, the week of Christmas, the temperature broke. No one knows why. The doctor said, "His natural immunity has fought off the pneumonia." In a greatly weakened condition, he came home for Christmas, very ill and confined to his bed most of the time.

While he was courageous, drawing upon his secure upbringing and his easygoing attitude, he was also resigned to his circumstances. But then what cancer patient isn't to some degree? What was he going to do about his illness?

When he returned to the hospital for checkups or for chemotherapy, he wanted to distance himself from the other children who were ill. When he underwent the radiation treatments, he looked around the underground room at all of the little gray-haired ladies and disease-ravaged men and said nothing. But he didn't need to communicate because his eyes said it all. When he was well enough to have regrets, he often referred to the real tragedy of the semester, the fact that he would have been trying out for basketball the day of his initial diagnosis.

Of all of the manifestations of the illness, the hair loss was the worst. Steve could take everything else because he could suffer behind closed doors, then come out pale but able to join his friends. Not so with the hair loss. At first there seemed no way to cover up the bald head, but the real problem was the fact that the hair loss meant he really *did* have cancer, and he really was in a life-threatening situation.

Probably one of the saddest nights during this time was the night I drove him out into the country to a beauty shop in my school district. I had heard that this beautician wanted to help shape wigs for cancer patients, and had had some success in doing so. If we went at night, no one would drop in at the shop. If we left Stephen's school district, there would be no chance that someone we knew would drop in and see a beautician refashioning a woman's wig for this very sensitive teenage boy.

Previously, we had tried the custom-made man's wig. It looked like a pile of hair that was twice the size of Stephen's head. He was almost consumed by it. We had tried the real hair, dyed-to-match variety. Nothing worked, so we were out in the country trying to locate a beautician who would help us. That she did. Her efforts far surpassed those of the hairpiece professionals. Stephen had a feathered wig that worked well enough that he could play tennis on the tennis team and not lose it. No schoolmate ever said a word, and the predicted wig snatching that other young cancer patients had experienced never happened to him.

Most of all, we kept the "public Steve" and the "private Stephen" separate. He went out of our home to meet with his friends. Then he came back home and threw his wig across the room, resting secure that no one would see the Stephen who had cancer.

Stephen's brother, Brian, twelve years old, visited friends as much as possible during the daylight hours. Later we realized he might have left the house because he feared he might "get it" too. Having health problems of his own which we knew nothing about, Brian simply didn't understand the disease but knew that everyone in town knew his brother was very ill. His nonchalance was betrayed when we saw his grades and finally noticed his escapes to the homes of friends. He later told us that someone in science class had told him that leukemia could kill Steve.

During those twenty-two days of December, I coped by recalling much of what I had learned in childhood. In the afternoons I would write unstructured poetry or simply look out the window over the Medical Center campus and recall other happier times.

We had a farm in Indiana, in an area known for its subterranean streams, sinks, and springs. Often we were surrounded by flood water, which sank within two hours of the heaviest rainfall. On this farm there existed a peacefulness and beauty on summer days when the trees proudly displayed their underskirts of silver maple leaves and the white trumpets of catalpas. Under this canopy of trees grew a pastureland of patches of grass overlaid with sagebrush and dewberries, the latter with prickly, briery vines that threatened to trip the most cautious of bare feet.

The midsummer air in the slight fold below the hill was often still, the kind of humid air on which sweat-bees and horseflies thrive. Consequently, the only respite from the summer heat was the cool basement under our house. It was in this unfinished coal bin of a basement, while cutting out movie star pictures from my aunt's discarded Photoplay magazines, that I relaxed from 2:00 PM or so until dinner each day.

By early evening, the combined scent of "barn" and that of alfalfa in various stages of curing mingled with aromas wafting out from the kitchen window. Inside, in degrees of preparation, were midsummer vegetable soup, Kentucky Wonder polebeans, roasting ears of corn, baked yeast bread, and pies of the fresh fruit of the season.

In full view of this busy kitchen, the catalpa trees bowed out with limbs excellently shaped for children's swings and tree climbing. Except for the time of the year when catalpa worms took up residence, those trees provided a pleasant bower of shade for the land just beyond the kitchen window; thus that shot of kitchen window frames my memory when I recall the farm.

Our house, built in the late 1920s, was the kind that World War II soldiers returned to. Fronted with a porch that ran its width, the white farm house was trimmed in dark hunter green around its windows and its foundation. This farmhouse was the perfect setting for a simple life lived out in farm chores, pleasantly supplemented with church and school activities.

When school began each August. I was not only one of the first ones on the school bus, but also the only elementary school student for several miles down the road. Providing my own entertainment while the older kids roughhoused in the back of the bus, I mentally rehearsed fantastic stories about each farm, stories I had heard as my parents and grandparents regularly visited on Sunday afternoons.

The long ride (seven miles one way) began with the circus-show farm next door to our place. Even though it was now an abandoned show farm, I pulled from my memory well preserved bits and pieces of stories I had heard about this winter quarters for circus animals. One barn had housed elephants, one boarded lions and tigers. Another shed held the circus dogs. What an exotic place! Imagine—those gilt and red circus wagons bound for the French Lick Show were filled with circus animals that boarded across the field from my house!

In the hillside just beyond the show farm bend, the springs gushed out of the ground and rushed down to the road. These openings in the hills were well marked by the occasional rusty cup hanging on a spring-side stake—a welcome sight for thirsty travelers.

This crystal-clear water fascinated me and set my imagination to work. Routinely, I thought how underneath our bus, the ground was not solid. Instead, it was composed of underground streams that wound their way through rocks and caverns. Many of these streams were fed by ground water that sank via sinkholes and caves. How fantastic and mysterious was all this network just under the road!

The main stream was called Lost River, and it rose to the surface only a few yards from our Orangeville schoolyard. Predictably, in heave rainfall, the dry bed streams around the area would swell with rain water that routinely overflowed the banks. Then the next morning much of that surface water was drained away like water from a tub when the plug is pulled.

Traveling along in the bus, I thought about subterranean structures, as the school bus added two, three, six children at each stop until the vehicle was overflowing with children from first to twelfth grades.

The background for the way my life has unfolded is incomplete unless I add to the stories of bus rides, show farms, and sinkholes, the description of my secret place reserved for deep reflection during my years between ages nine and twelve.

To the right of our house and pond, the terrain rose sharply into a very steep hill. On top of this hill was a black walnut tree with sprawling branches that had sprouted relatively low to the ground. Each summer evening I climbed the fence that joined in that tree corner, and from that barbed wire I could take one big step into the lowest limb of the tree.

I came to this tree high above the world so I could fantasize about what might be going on beyond the fences of our farm. Certainly it was from this perch that I dreamed about my future family of "ten" children, and my beautiful horse farm planned around what I had seen on our trip down to Lexington one summer. My white-columned house at the end of the tree-lined lane would barely be visible from the main road. Thus, each evening, I thought about my future and about larger things than daily farm chores.

From this walnut tree high above my childhood, I never saw negatives in my future. Why should I? Always I saw a gradual progression of success and happiness.

In early January 1979, on his third extended stay in the hospital, Stephen's body balked. He was reacting to one of the drugs in his protocol. As the doctors ruled out first one drug and then another as being the troublemaker, we waited, very concerned, because all of these drugs made up the chemotherapy he needed. Not one was unnecessary for his disease to remain in remission. Finally the culprit was located. Bactrim at that time was used alongside the chemotherapy to help prevent the often-inevitable pneumonia. Stephen was reacting to the Bactrim. Fortunately, it was not a part of the chemical mix needed to suppress the disease and could be withdrawn.

No sooner had we resolved one problem than another arose. Stephen had developed histoplasmosis. While histoplasmosis is treatable in patients who have no other disease, it could be a serious disease in a patient whose resistance is worn and eroded by high dosages of chemotherapy. Certainly, the chemotherapy that was keeping the leukemia in check could not be discontinued in order to administer six to eight weeks of a daily drip procedure of an antibiotic to rid the body of the histoplasmosis. Even though the oncologist did not exactly spell out the prognosis as we later heard it, we knew there was serious trouble brewing as a second and a third histo-titer were ordered, and everyone on the hospital team anxiously awaited the results.

The histoplasmosis development was really the only one that was never spelled out to Stephen until the whole incident had passed. Barry and I were told the histo-titers were being run and that the disease could be very serious or even fatal because the chemotherapy would have to be discontinued in order to treat the histoplasmosis. The body probably could not endure both procedures at once.

Meanwhile I dared to check my medical encyclopedia for the description of the course histoplasmosis follows. Knowing well that our oncologist had cautioned against this practice of amateurly diagnosing disease, I forged ahead. Fortunately, somewhere in the back of my mind, I did hear him warn that medical books especially designed for the layperson often contain information that is at least two years out of date. After all, it does take at least two years to publish a book, even a book of the latest findings in medical research. Nonetheless, I decided to read on. Histoplasmosis was defined as a serious fungal disease, resembling tuberculosis, that primarily affects the lungs of men. It is most common in the central United States.

Very soon I concluded that we were now fighting the environment. Great! All we needed was an additional enemy. I decided this histoplasmosis came from the excavation done near our house the previous spring, for the condition sometimes develops in people who live near freshly dug dirt. Then, again, the culprit could be the pop can collection. I had often lamented at Stephen's practice of finding in a ditch beside the road "the one can I don't have for the collection." After all, who knew the history of that can? How many germs lived therein? In fact, all summer long I had washed and scalded each can by means of a sterilizing process fit for a canning factory.

Now that I was searching the environment for the source of each problem we encountered, I was searching my memory for life and death cases I had heard reviewed at the hospital lab where I had worked years before. In this period, the following account surfaced and became a part of my journal.

Ironically, when I was seventeen years old, my formal introduction to environmentally induced death occurred in the same location that had provided me with such fantastic imaginings as a child. The setting was a cave, a part of an underground network of springs, sinks, and a lost river. Yes, it had been this network that so enthralled me as I rode the school bus year after year and looked out the window as the countryside rolled by.

It was 8:00 PM when my boyfriend and I, both seventeen years old, decided we could not drive the car beyond the mulberry tree about 200 feet from the lane that led up to my house. Since shortly after 5:00 that Sunday evening, rain had been falling in torrents, and my house was completely surrounded by rapidly rising water that appeared to be in search of a stream to follow. Drivers from the area had long since discontinued attempts to go through the water to reach the gravel road that proceeded on west to a small country community called Hindostan.

As my father swept the flashlight from side to side, warning us not to try to drive through the rushing waters, we decided I would spend the night in town, eight miles away. In fact, we had turned to drive away when an approaching pick-up truck charged up to the water's edge. Familiar with the occasional rise in waters around our house, I cautioned him not to try to drive through.

However, I did not have to tell him, for he had already decided to leave the truck and wade, swim, whatever he had to do to move across this flooded low land. Hurriedly, he explained to us that at 5:00 that afternoon, almost an hour before the rainstorm had hit, two young Indiana University spelunkers (cavers, if you wish) had entered a well-known, privately owned cave. This cave was unusual in that it was like a hole in the ground and not a room set into the rocky hillside. This characteristic of the cave could mean disaster for these lost cavers. All of the hills had emptied flood water into the valley and, therefore, into the cave's entrance. He explained that he had volunteered to lead a group of rescue workers to the approximate location of the cave, and expert diving teams would try to locate the opening—not to mention try to go inside to rescue the young men.

Not wanting to interfere with the rescue, we wished him success and headed into town, eight miles east. As we drove away, I could not help but wonder what my parents would think when all of the rescue workers pulled up to the water's edge and then tried to cross the water. Surely the lights from the lanterns held high above their heads would create an eerie sight when viewed from our front window on the hill above the water.

Little did I know that during the night our house would become the command post for the Red Cross and for every major newspaper in the tri-state area. In fact, at 4:00 AM with only a flashlight to guide them, my dad led an out-of-the-area newspaper reporter through the rain-soaked woods. Oblivious to the wet tree limbs slapping him in the face, this reporter wanted to be first to record the story of the rescue efforts to save two students' lives. Soon everyone in the area saw that this was no ordinary news story, for it had all of the elements of adventure, horror, bravery, cunning and use of survival techniques that build unforgettable drama into a story.

For the next three days, helicopters brought in news reporters and took away news reporters. Speculation covered such topics as the unusual terrain under our farm and in this area. Geologists revealed that we sat on a honeycomb network of subterranean waterways that usually took any ground water and fed it to an underground lost river. A network of sinkholes on our farm and the neighboring farms, plus springs and caves, added to the intrigue of the story. Surely this area was unlike any other in the Midwest.

Then there were hypotheses posed as to what survival strategies the two men may be using inside the cave. Expert cavers said, trained as spelunkers are, they would undoubtedly be high on ledges in the largest room of the cave. Even if the water rose to near the ceiling of the cave, there would still be air pockets, and the men were positioning themselves on the ledges to benefit from that air. What a mental picture I carried of two men clawing their way to the safety of a ledge and tilting their heads to a certain angle in order to breathe from the few pockets of air in the whole cave!

I shall never forget that Tuesday evening two days into the rescue mission when my family went over to the hillside above the cave and waited with the families of the cavers and neighbors of ours from the surrounding area. An expert had our attention when he described what the men must have seen when the water had entered the cave two days earlier. Certainly it had not been a trickle of rain water that had inched its way through the cave. Instead, all of the water of the bottom land around had rushed into that cave's entrance. When the wall of water had approached the men, it would have sounded like a freight train traveling through a mountainside tunnel. The water would have rushed ceiling high, not the gradual rising one would expect. The men would have had to make some very quick decisions in order to move to the highest ledges near the source of oxygen. How horrible!

As we grew silent after hearing that bit of information, I moved away from everyone else, as though I needed to privately digest what was happening, but soon my attention turned to the two-year-old daughter of one of the trapped cavers. She was toddling along, picking the tops of wild flowers growing on a flat area above the stony cave's entrance. Her presence made the whole scene even more heart-rending.

Late that evening as we returned home, we realized that the mystery would be resolved the next day, for one of the rescue team members had explained that a person cannot live long without food and water. Certainly, water would be the first demand, and drinking the contaminated river water would create a whole new set of health problems.

What a troubled heart I had as I went to bed that night! Actually, I did not have long to lie awake and think about the rescue, for 6:00 AM I was pulling out of our driveway in my dad's 1957 Chevy to go to the county hospital lab where I worked as a lab assistant.

The fact that the lab was deserted was not unusual, for the early morning hours were usually spent with lab technicians rushing through the medical-surgical unit to draw blood in preparation for the patients' scheduled surgeries.

Enjoying the quiet atmosphere, I read the stack of orders for the day. Next, I wandered over to the sink. Since I was a part-time employee, I usually washed bottles and equipment throughout the day. I could see that the sinks were already full and waiting for me to arrive.

In the double sinks were two very heavy aluminum cauldrons with doctor's orders beside each one no patient name appeared on the orders, but there was no mistaking who the patients had been, for the orders for processing this tissue were clearly labeled:

HUMAN LUNGS: Prepare Path Report to determine if river water was cause of death.

Death . . . that was the subject of the year. Everything we did pointed to death. Who were we fooling anyway? There was only one way this illness in Stephen would end. Because of this certainty much of what I did and said was related to death. My mind turned in to the driveways of a hundred funeral homes throughout the day.

The person who is going through a crisis always mentally or physically returns "home" to look for answers to the dilemma. Here I was in a large city hospital, yet was thinking of all I had learned at home and in the county where I grew up.

Orange County is distinguished by its topography: hilly terrain, red clay dirt, mineral springs, the Lost River, and "salt of the earth" people. A predominately rural county, Orange County offers little to farmers who are looking for high crop yields. Only those who live along rivers and own the "bottom land" produce the crops comparable to those of their neighbors to the north.

Perfectly accessorized with mineral springs, the Carlsbad of America in West Baden, the county, for the most part has never been able to capitalize on the wealth of natural resources unless the area also ran major casinos and gambling dens as in the 1920s and 1930s. even being the headquarters of seven large circus companies in the 1920s was not sufficient to produce significant widespread wealth in the area. Plus, the people are largely unimpressed with celebrity and wealth; therefore, the residents of Orange County have resisted nourishing a resort for outsiders.

All of my life I have marveled at the cache of that karst terrain, the unpublished journals, the furnishings dating to the early 1800s, the collections of Indian artifacts, the natural springwater, the wealth of knowledge about the lumber industry and wood products, the stacks of quilts, the untouched local folklore—the list goes on—all were and are a part of Orange County, Indiana. And it was into this red soil of this undeveloped area that I mentally searched for roots to hold onto as we dealt with Stephen's cancer.

A turn-of-the century baptism at Lost River. Perhaps some of my relatives are there.

Judy McCart at age three.

The Methodist church at Orangeville attended by my family. Here the McCart family sat in two rows. Family activities centered at the church.

Lost River today—at flood stage.

Barry and I were married in 1963 in Orleans United Methodist Church.

Two weeks after the various tests for the histoplasmosis were run, we heard the results of the later titers. We were flabbergasted at these results, as were the doctors. The histoplasmosis had retreated. It was gone! Later in the week of that report, in a pediatric oncology meeting in Toronto, Stephen's doctor presented this unusual case of "disappearing" histoplasmosis in the cancer patient. All of the pediatric oncologists who heard that Stephen's histoplasmosis had disappeared immediately agreed it was unheard of the histoplasmosis had retreated in a patient with this type of cancer with this particular protocol for chemotherapy.

Whatever the traditional course was, this disease in Stephen was gone. Undoubtedly, there are some aspects of every disease that completely baffle every doctor. Histoplasmosis might not merely disappear, but something happened to it, for the disease no longer appeared on the repeated titers that were run thereafter.

Celebration was in order. Steve had survived six months of the most aggressive protocol of chemotherapy and radiation a person with his body weight could tolerate. He donned his wig, and we were soon on our way to Ft. Myers Beach, Florida.

Even though over the course of sixteen more months of chemotherapy, bone marrows and spinal taps, there was normalcy, which included such activities as Stephen's playing on the high school tennis team, there were days when he lay lifeless. And there were evenings when we made the late-night trips to Riley Hospital's emergency room for unexplained excruciating pain in his face and nose or ulcerations inside his mouth or high fevers or double vision or bleeding during vomiting after chemotherapy or several of the above all at once. Fortunately, as weeks turned into months, these episodes were farther and farther apart. Normal days were returning—as normal as our lives would ever be again, yet this evil disease still hung over us. He would die—fifty percent of children with acute lymphocytic leukemia did die in 1980. I had known the stalker; he had shadowed my life. It was only a matter of time.

It was thirteen months after the diagnosis of leukemia in Stephen when Dr. Peter Marshall came to a church in our neighborhood for a three-day evangelistic meeting. Recalling how as a teenager I had read and reread the love story of his parents, *A Man Called Peter,* how I had found counsel in *To Live Again* after my father had died, and had loved reading all of his mother's books, I decided to go to hear this son of Catherine and the late Dr. Peter Marshall.

After a day of cleaning the house and grading school papers, I threw on my coat on this very cold January evening and headed for the church. So nonchalant was my attendance that evening, I did not even put on the usual "church clothes." I decided I would slip in on the back row and leave immediately following the service. I have to admit something here. it is true that my faith was all but nonexistent at this point. The mood of those first moments, when my husband and I had learned of our son's illness and questioned God, had not altered. God was not the loving Father that I had thought he was.

Taking my seat in the back of the sanctuary, I felt secure in that the service had already begun, and besides, I could leave anytime I wanted. These thirteen months of no communication with God had actually caused me to doubt the sanity of spending so much time in church anyway, for Barry and I were living proof that God does not remember His own.

No sooner had I tucked away a few negative thoughts than I noticed that the singing was unusually spirited. I reasoned that everyone in attendance was like me, in awe of the late Dr. Peter Marshall and his wife Catherine, and they were really singing in memory and honor of them. Or maybe these people had foreknowledge of the topic of the three-day meeting, which was a call for American Christians to wake up and lead this nation again. Regardless of the reason, I was strangely moved by the spirit of the service from the moment I settled in on the back row.

Furthermore, from the first idea woven into Dr. Marshall's sermon until the close, I knew I would seek his counsel about my lack of help from God in this matter of our son's illness. It was as though all of my years of devouring books written by his parents had prepared me to be on the same wavelength with a son they had also taught.

Today, as I reflect, I suppose that God worked though Dr. Marshall on that January night for two reasons: God knew I would leave my warm house on this cold night and be exceptionally receptive to hearing the son of ones I had long admired, and most importantly, this man was totally covered by his own personal prayers and the corporate prayers of the people in the church. Plus, from a practical point of view, Dr. Marshall and I were the same age, had our Bibles marked heavily in the judgment sections, and both knew about the fear one has when faced with losing a child. All in all, it was no coincidence that I attended that service in January 1980.

An hour after my entrance, I prepared to be the first person to go forward for prayer. Dr. Marshall closed the service and proceeded to meet with each of us in the order in which we had come to the altar. Therefore, when he came to me and asked if he might pray with me, I choked out, "My son is going to die of leukemia. What am I going to do?" Without a moment's hesitation, he responded, "Stay here. I want to talk with you." I felt chilled. It seemed that he, too, had no answers for me.

As I explain my negative reaction to this today, the reader has to remember that since our son's diagnosis, people had reacted to our presence in very strange ways. Those who had appeared to be the churched people in our midst had run to hide when we came about. Those who did not have God in their lives were the caring ones who repeatedly asked us if there was anything they could do. Thus, the evil forces in my mind interpreted what I thought I saw. Ministers didn't know any more about this early death business than we did. And people really didn't care too much unless the person who was ill was their loved one. It was with that viewpoint that I sat in the pew and waited as Dr. Marshall went on to the next person who sought prayer or counsel.

As he turned away to speak with the fifteen or so seeking prayer, I was thinking he was reacting to my dilemma in the same way as everyone else. In fact, I was reminded of the Little League mother who had stopped me in the grocery store to inquire "about Steve," then nervously, she began fingering the Pampers diapers nearby simply because she needed to distance herself from my answer to her inquiry. Never mind that she had no infants or grandchildren in her life. Now tonight this person who had shown such promise in understanding my dilemma had elected to pray with others in order to escape "bad news."

I sat there thinking, "As always, one thing is certain: no one lingers around a conversation that has turned to the subject of cancer in children."

Yet for once I could not muster the strength to be angry nor cynical about what I perceived as a brush off. As I waited, all of my thoughts centered on the fact that tonight I had reached the end of my strength. Yes, I would stay to talk with him because I was unable to continue as I was going. My resources were spent.

Reminding everyone to return the following evening, Dr. Marshall said his goodbyes to the others who had waited to talk with him and secure book autographs; then he turned back to me. As he turned, he said, "Your Bible is marked in all of the wrong places. Let me guess . . . you have all of the passages on the "do nots" marked. You have often pondered over the sections on the wrath of God. Right? Yours is a Revelation-geared belief?"

By now, since he had hardly made reference to childhood leukemia, I was convinced that he had confused my question with that of someone else, and nonetheless, I sensed I was indulging him by saying, "Yes, it is. I grew up in a church where every altar-call included an admonition that we might be killed on the way home if we did not repent of our sins before we left." Then I added, "How did you know?"

"Because until recently my own Bible was marked in the same way; there, it was easy to recognize the same in another," he answered. "Then I took another look at what the Bible was saying to me. Now here is what I want you to do. go home, and, starting tonight using your concordance, mark every reference to God's love for you. Then when you have completed that assignment, write to me, at this address" (he wrote on a small card) "and tell me what you have discovered."

With that, he prayed for my enabling and sent me on my way. Oblivious to the few who were preparing the building for the next morning service, I was certain I would find what I needed as I conducted this search. Surely, he had sensed that I was exhausted with carrying a burden about which I could do nothing. Here was a person who was going to help our family.

Undoubtedly led by the Spirit of God, I literally marched out of the church into the deep-freeze of an Indiana January and never looked back, never questioned the fact that Dr. Peter Marshall had not answered my question at all. "What am I going to do when my son dies?" Certainly when God gave the message, it was very clear and pre-packed. I knew I had heard a word from HIM. I also knew that Dr. Marshall had prayed for guidance for the evening.

Was I ever focused! For over a year I had wrestled "with the angel at the foot of the ladder that leads up to God." I knew that on this night I had been given instructions on how to make the first move up that ladder.

Within the week, I knew why Dr. Marshall had suspected that I had overlooked the verses about God's love. He could see that I believed I was responsible for, had somehow caused my son's illness, and that now I was being punished.

Had I prepared a printout of the assignment Dr. Marshall gave me and used it in a Bible Study, it undoubtedly would have looked much like the following:

Re: The Love of God   Date of Study: _________

Situation: ___________   Your Name: _________

1. He loves me so much He has planned my inheritance.

    A. II Corinthians 6:18: I am **God's daughter**.
       I shall inherit what a daughter would inherit.

    B. Haggai 2:23: God will make me **His signet ring**.
       (Consider the value of this piece of jewelry found in the king's jewelry box.)

    C. a. John 14:2: Because of His great love for me, He is **preparing a mansion for me**. b. How will I locate this place? (John 14:4)
       I will know the way. (God tells me exactly how to make the journey no matter how difficult.)

    D. Jeremiah 29:11: He knows the *plans* He has for me.

    E. Psalm 47:4 Because of His great love for me, He chooses the *inheritance for me, the pride of Jacob, whom He loved.*

    F. Revelation 14:1: He loves me so much He wants others to know I am His. He has placed His *mark* on me.

    G. Psalm 139:16: All my days were written *in His book.*

2. He loves me so much He protects me.

   A. Zechariah 2:8: He that touches me, touches *the apple of His eye.*

   B. Isaiah 43:4 I am *precious* in His sight.

   C. Deuteronomy 33:12 The Lord *covers* to His heart.

   D. Isaiah 40:11: He carries me *close to His heart.*

   E. Psalms 33:18: Because He loves me like a parent loves a child, He keeps an *eye on me.*

   F. Psalm 34:7. I have a *brush* of God on my life because angels encamp around me.

   G. Hosea 11:3-4: Like a loving parent who stands behind a toddler and holds the child's hands as she toddles, God leads me, His beloved, with *cords of love.*

   H. Psalm 17:8: He hides me in the shadow of his *wings.*

   I. Isaiah 49:16: The Lord says, "I have engraved you on the *palms of my hands . . .."*

3. He loves me so much that he feeds me.

   A. John 15:4: Remain attached to *Him,* and I will be fruitful.

   B. Hosea 11:4: He bends down and **feeds me.**

4. He loves me so much that He sticks close by throughout the night and stays beside me in sickness and trouble.

   A. Psalm 63:6: In His love, He is with me in *the watches of the night.*

   B. Zephaniah 3:17: He lulls me with his love. He takes great *delight* in me. He *lulls* me with singing.

   C. Psalm 42:8: All night long His song is with me— this song is a prayer to the Lord of my life.

   D. Psalm 143:8: Dear God, let the morning bring me word of your unfailing *love.*

   E. Psalm 147:3: He heals the *brokenhearted*.

5. He loves me so much He oversaw my creation.

   A. Psalm 139:14: I am **fearfully** and **wonderfully** made.

   B. Psalm 119:73: His **hands** created me.

6. He loves me so much He forgives me of sins; the same sins that He cannot look upon—for He is holy.

   A. Psalm 103:12 He swept away **my offenses**.

   B. Micah 7:19 Because He loves me, He hurls my wrong doings **out to sea**.

   C. Isaiah 44:22 He lovingly says to me, "Return to me, for **I have returned to you.**"

   D. II Samuel 12:24 He forgives sins that are so great that they involve murder, lies and all types of evil. God even loved a son **Solomon** born to the unfaithful David and Bathsheba. He forgives any and all of my sins.

   E. Isaiah 38:17 In God's love He kept me from the **pit of destruction**; He has put all of my **sins** behind his back.

   F. John 3:16 God loves me so much that He gave **His own son** and a ransom to re deem me.

   G. Ephesians 2:5 God **loved me** before I had acknowledged that I loved Him.

7. He loves me so much that He disciplines me to be the best that I can be.

   A. Psalms 139:5 He **hems** me in as a parent sets boundaries so the child will be safe. He has laid his hand upon me.

   B. Proverbs 3:12 God disciplines **those He loves**.

   C. Hebrews 12:8 Anyone who belongs to God is **disciplined** as a son. He is the parent.

8. He loves me so much that He lovingly guides me through each day.

A. Psalms 42:8: By day He directs me with ***His love, at night his song is with me***.

B. Psalm 23:4 He will even guide me unto ***death***.

C. Psalm 4:6 He leads me by the light of his ***face***.

D. Isaah 30:21: because He loves me, He gives me signs along my paths which will say, "This is ***the way***."

9. He loves me so much He wants to walk beside me, like ***a brother***.

   A. Proverbs 18:24 He is a friend who sticks closer than ***a brother***.

   B. Matthew 11:29 He wants me to stand beside Him on the other side of the ***yoke;*** so that the two of us will pull my daily load of life together.

10. He loves me so that all mankind cannot comprehend how great is His love for me.

    A. I John 3:1: How great is the **love He has lavished** on us.

    B. Ephesians 3:18: My aim is to have the power to grasp how ***wide*** and ***high*** is the love of Christ and to ***know*** his love surpasses ***knowledge***.

    C. Matthew 4:6: The Lord lovingly gives His ***angels*** charge concerning those He loves.

Now when I retreat into my former "He loves me—He Loves me not" attitude, I pull out these passages and soon conclude:

HE LOVES ME!

For months, actually two years, Peter Marshall discussed via letters the love of God with me. Yes, he did finally answer that question posed on the first night of my pilgrimage through the passages on the love of God. Or did I find the answer in those passages? Who knows, but somehow I learned that I would rest in the love of God. I would know that this child was also being comforted by this love of God. I would know God's will for this child contained the only future I could ever want for him, too.

In His faithfulness, God made His presence known in wonderful ways. One such avenue for His revelation came through my sponsorship of a high school Huddle of Girls for Fellowship of Christian Athletes. Seemingly, I had a perfect excuse to pass such responsibility onto another adult. But God was even saving me the trouble and time that I may have spent on worry so those hours could be used in serving Him through Fellowship of Christian Athletes.

Through the course of the five years of sponsorship of this Girl's Huddle of forty-five high-school girls, our group was actively involved at every level: local, state and national. The wonderful fringe benefit of my long hours of after-school work was the encouragement I received from the FCA students, both girls and boys, the other sponsors in the area, and the messages of the wonderful speakers who travel the country following the Christian Athletes.

While my motivation for my service does not sound so pure, now that I analyze it, I feel certain that one in the throes of sorrow and desperation can do no greater thing than serve those who could benefit. In my case, as a high school teacher, the sponsorship of a life-changing organization designed to fulfill God's purposes in each life was the position for me to fill. Today, when I see former students with two or three children in tow, rarely do I hear them praise my technique for proper pronoun usage. They usually refer to lessons learned in Fellowship of Christian Athletes' meetings.

Certainly, in my opinion, the person who is suddenly thrust into a family crisis should seek a position of serving others in God's name. I don't think I was fully aware of that truth at that time, but there I was in my place anyway. And certainly, I got more than I gave.

One experience of group support that resulted from my sponsorship of FCA occurred at a Fall Retreat. The girls were completing several rounds of athletic contests; the sponsors had gone ahead of them to prepare for the evening's activities. As we waited for the last group of athletes, one of the sponsors turned to me and said, "Judy, give us an update on Steve's situation." Aware that they knew all of the background, I simply said, "All is well; however, the doctors want to cut his chemotherapy protocol short. They suspect the patients receive more chemotherapy than is needed. Since the chemotherapy destroys good cells as well as the bad, the doctors feel they should start cutting back on the number of months of treatment. Steve will be in that first class of patients (1980) on which to experiment on that theory."

Expecting the other sponsors to comment on such a theory, I was surprised when Janet blurted out, "Mildred, is this the boy I've been praying for these last two years?" It was such a candid moment; I shall never forget it. Actually such comfort and affirmation were typical of the kinds of support I received from these loyal servants of God. I had sent school pictures of Stephen to Mildred, a prayer warrior. I knew she would circulate them among other prayer warriors. She did. She worked quietly. Then on this day, two years later, a woman I had never met announced that she had been praying for my son in her daily prayers. She had faithfully prayed for someone she had never met. Even as I write, I marvel at such faithfulness.

Involved in every possible type of program available for Bible Study and Christian Growth, I was given the tools necessary for survival during a difficult time. What would have happened if I had simply folded my hands and sat waiting for the next phase of the fast merry-go-round ride one takes with a child with cancer?

All experiences have their own by-products to contend with. This situation is no different. Soon, very soon, after we had begun checking our son in and out of the hospital, consulting a trail of oncologists and professionals whose expertise was needed, we began to receive unusual mail.

Apparently, a printout of all people with newly diagnosed cancer circulates among people who would exploit such a situation for we received form letters addressed to parents whose children suffer from terminal illnesses.

One man sent us a piece of cloth of his bathrobe. Placing this small square of cloth under our pillow, we would be assured of the continued prayers of this man for our son. Such a practice would guarantee that the cancer would go into remission forever. Of course, we were to send money to this man in exchange for his prayers. While we had been in Christian circles all of our lives, we had never heard his name nor have we heard it since that mailing. Such communications are very disturbing to parents of children with serious illnesses.

One lady whose methods many would consider extreme, however, politely asked if she might pray for and anoint Stephen. After hearing the story of her past, I somehow concluded that her anointing would cause no harm. She quietly slipped into the living room of my sister-in-law's house, and in ten minutes, after a fervent prayer and anointing with oil, she slipped out with no fanfare at all. My husband and I did not know her, nor have we seen her since.

Even before she began to pray, I knew God was very near to us. Words cannot describe those moments of prayer; actually, words are unnecessary, I really don't recall anything she included in her prayer, for I was talking with God myself. After she left, I knew that God had worked through this woman, I felt like Isaiah when he said he saw the Lord lifted up with His train filling the whole temple (Isaiah 6:1), I saw Him lifted up with His train filling the whole house. Often, we look back to that day and wonder If the healing took place then. Perhaps it did. Whatever happened, we know we were in the presence of God.

Family members also stood by with great encouragement. I shall always remember how my grandmother, age eighty-four, responded to the news that her great-grandson had leukemia. Grandmother rallied to the occasion more quietly and efficiently than any of us. Perhaps somewhere back in the 1920s and 1930s, she had learned perseverance through the adversity of losing a young husband and subsequently rearing four girls on not much more than what her farm could produce. As A. W. Tozier said, "It is doubtful if God can use anyone whom He has not first broken."

Grandmother . . . I began to see how her influence in my life had stemmed from her Orange County roots, yet it is difficult to explain how my grandmother's influences, attitudes her life helped to bolster me in this trying time. She was born two miles form the valley of West Baden–French Lick–on a large farm that was the envy of farmers of the area. In Orange County, one must own land along a river in order to enjoy high yields from crops. The Stackhouse farm where Grandmother grew up had that rich ground. Corn, sorghum, and hay were the crops. There were huge gardens, too. Hogs, turkeys, hens and dairy cows roamed the pastures. Grandmother, thus, enjoyed some privilege since she was so well provided for and since her father was the powerful county school trustee. In those days the county school trustee wielded seemingly unlimited power. Due to opportunities which undoubtedly grew from her influential father's activities, she went to work in a "branch bank" in the lobby of the celebrated domed West Baden Hotel. In 1912, for a girl to work anywhere was unusual. Certainly Grandmother was in a very sophisticated employment in one of the most talked-about casino hotels in the world. Soon she married, had the four daughters and then suddenly her husband died. Some people marked the start of the Great Depression with the fall of the stock market; Grandmother started that era with the death of her husband. As she began to gather berries and serve her children popcorn for cereal, she unknowingly began to teach me resilience long before my birth. I'll call it Lost River resilience because it came form the Orange County variety of perseverance into which I was born.

So now, Grandmother was coming through for me once again. One hundred miles south of us and unable to make hospital calls she answered the call to help raise funds for cancer research by "squirreling away" craft supplies for the coming winter of hibernation.

Day after day, from December to July, Grandmother sewed, glued, wrapped, wove, tied, whatever the directions called for. In short, she quickly grasped a principle that all must learn. The questions is, "What can I do?" not "What I wish I could do to change this very bad situation." Imagine our astonishment when we realized that Grandmother had furnished over one-third of the items sold in the Riley Cancer Research for Children's annual Indianapolis citywide bazaar the following July. By harnessing the energy that would otherwise have been expended in worry and directing it into an activity that she could do, she weathered difficult times, as well as helped all children who suffer with cancer.

By the time we completed the initial intense round of chemotherapy, the ten continuous days of radiation, the serious twenty-two-day bout with pneumonia, a reaction to the Bactrium drug, and histoplasmosis that came and went, a whole year had passed. We had finally come to the time when, for several days at a time, there were no late-night emergency room visits. As in all things when the rush appears to be over and the survivor has time to reflect on what has happened, her formerly strong approach becomes weakened sometimes to the point of emotional collapse. I could see that I was not nearly as prepared to rise to the emergency one year after the diagnosis as I had been initially. Yet I was now beginning to tap into new-found, God-given resources instead of relying on my own strength.

It was summertime, nineteen months after Stephen's diagnosis of leukemia, when I took him to the hospital for complete physical exam, including the usual bone marrow test and the spinal tap. Even though his bones, because of the chemotherapy, had thinned by now, the bone marrow test was not at all pleasant, but, according to him, not as painful as in the early days of treatment. More painful was the spinal tap. Therefore, the day's visit was especially dreaded.

As we drove along a busy side road to reach the Interstate, I noticed that my formerly active Stephen was very quiet. Knowing what he might be thinking, I asked, "Are you worried about the spinal tap?"

"Yes. No. actually, I'm remembering that I wasn't all that ill on the day they found the leukemia in the first place. They could find something wrong today."

I was smothering, but from months of practice, I managed to look straight ahead. No amount of control was keeping me from feeling panicky however, and I knew our appointment in the hospital's hematology clinic was scheduled in a half an hour. With Barry out of town, I was the only available driver for this trip.

Perspiring and feeling very weak, I prayed a prayer without even forming the words on my lips, and certainly without closing my eyes! This inaudible prayer may have been one of the most sincere prayers of my life, yet I was somewhat surprised at its content.

No sooner had I added the final. "Amen" than the car became entangled with a large metal sandwich-board sign announcing the upcoming opening of a new McDonald's restaurant. Never mind that in order to pick up that sign, my car had changed lanes, left the road, jumped a ditch, and landed in the appropriate lane. As we traveled several feet, we heard the loudest clattering noise ever as, bit by bit, the sign disentangled itself from our left front bumper. Also for several feet, I tried to correct the direction of the car, swerve to avoid other cars, and start on our way again. Then without anticipating my reaction, I began to laugh. What a hoot! These few seconds had been some of the funniest of my lifetime, for I alone knew the content of my prayer request. I had prayed for distractions, and did I ever get them! Enjoying this unlikely source of entertainment for no more than a total of seconds, I had failed to share these thoughts with the pale-faced son beside me.

Half paralyzed with fear, this fifteen-year-old who, like many fifteen-year-old sons, was already wondering if women should be in situations that involved responsibility, blurted out an exasperated, "MOM?!!"

Partially because of the release from intense anxiety only moments before and certainly because this development was hilarious, I laughed and could not stop. Not seeing the humor, he continued, "What are you trying to do, kill us?" that, too, struck me as funny. Tears rolled down my face as I laughed.

As much as he was trying to maintain the attitude that moms cannot drive, Stephen finally could not avoid seeing the humor in this situation. He, too, began to laugh. Then he began to recap what I had just done. "We went across three lanes of traffic and back across those same three lanes of traffic dragging a large metal McDonald's sign, which we had picked up under the left bumper as we traveled several feet in a ditch." His conclusion: "Next time I will be riding with Dad!"

As we laughed, the miles clipped away. Soon we arrived at Riley Hospital for Children in Indianapolis. I am certain that Stephen had heard and understood what I said when I explained that prayer must have set the chain reaction into motion. However, he was enjoying the story too much on the level of logical thinking to allow for the supernatural aspect. He simply responded, "No wonder we went oof the road–you had your eyes closed."

Giggling as we went, we soon took the exit ramp to the hospital, parked in the garage, and stumbled in through the side door, laughing every step of the way. Such joyful patients oncologists rarely see. No doubt they were happy to witness laughter, and soon our laughter had become contagious, for the whole staff was enjoying the retelling of our story.

Unusually lighthearted after months of anxiety, pain, and real misery, Stephen retained this distraction from the business at hand, even as he doubled up for the spinal tap. In fact, as the fluid was extracted, he said to the doctor, "My moped bike is safe compared to riding with Mom!" I looked at my son. He sounded like his old charging-around self.

Meanwhile, I pondered all that had happened, I marveled at the genius of God. What timing He has! What protection He had given to us and to the cars nearby! Best of all, the sign was no longer needed, for the restaurant opened later that week. While God doesn't go around causing car accidents, He can and may use those that occur to His and our benefit.

Remembering to be thankful in all things, my thoughts turned to thanksgiving. If for no other reason, I would be thankful for moments of grace and relief in a very intense, emotion-filled routine of undergoing tests during the course of a serious illness. I would praise God forever.

Certainly, the answers to prayer that have made the most impact upon my life have come when my own resources were spent. Yet even in the most exhausted state, I always prayed my prayers with great faith that God would answer them. Following the example in II Chronicles 20:12, I prayed, "O our God . . . we do not know what to do, but our eyes are on you."

SLEEP, SWEET SLEEP

Actually, the twenty-four-hour reactions to chemotherapy had become a part of every month by now–a year-and-a-half into the chemotherapy. Winter had set in, and November, often a month of trouble for us, had come and gone. We were starting the new year.

The protocol for Stephen's chemotherapy, carefully formulated between Riley Hospital and Stanford Medical School, had been the maximum strength based upon his body weight. Actually, only an hour after the diagnosis, we had been given a choice as to the strength of the chemotherapy for his protocol. Since we concluded that understanding strength of chemotherapy was not our expertise, we simply asked, "If he were your son, what protocol would you choose?"

On one particular occasion, Steve's white blood count, usually dangerously lowered by the chemotherapy, was sufficiently elevated to withstand the treatment in its full strength. However, the resultant effects of that treatment struck with a fury.

Because I am very much a night person and my husband is very much a day person, as I have said, early-on we decided to sit beside Stephen according to the schedules our bodies normally favor.

One particular night vigil at home proceeded as follows: It was now past midnight, one hour into my watch and six hours since Stephen's violent bouts of vomiting had begun. In the moments when the nausea would subside for only ten minutes' respite, I comforted myself with silently recalling parts of hymns, verses, anything I could remember. I remember the Psalm 63:6 was a favorite at that time:

On my bed I remember you;
I think of you
Through the watches of the night.
Because you are my help,
I sing in the shadow of your wings.
My soul clings to you;
Your right hand upholds me.

Often as I sat beside the bed, I became greatly comforted immediately before the situation took a turn for the worst. God had a way of preparing me. Tonight was no exception.

Suddenly, at approximately 2:30 am, the bouts of vomiting changed, for now all I disposed of was bright red blood. As Steve quieted into a few minutes of rest, my mind began to float through all that I had known about leukemia and hemorrhaging. In a picture I carried in my mind, I saw the left side of another bed of a young boy in that small county hospital where I had worked sixteen years earlier. Across the room on the walls of the bathroom was a fine spray of bright red. Then I remembered the hospital gossip a few days later when this sixteen-year-old boy died. "Didn't his mother know he has been dying for months? How could she go into shock when she saw him move closer to death every day?"

Returning to the present and hurrying to leave the past memories behind, I realized the vomiting had once again continued. Again I disposed of what I thought was a large amount of bright red blood.

With Stephen settled once more, I hurried to our bedroom and awakened Barry to tell him I could not continue my shift of sitting with Stephen. Normally, the unexpected interruption of the other's rest was to be avoided if at all possible. However, I was falling apart. Accustomed to a household that revolved around the patient even in the earliest hours of morning, Barry was up and on his way down the hall, no questions asked.

Meanwhile, once alone, I literally dropped to the floor of the bedroom, and face down on the floor, I prayed, "Dear Lord, just for the next few hours, please let Stephen sleep. It is so scary when this happens at night, Lord. Please. Just until morning."

A slant of dim light fell across my face as I lay on the bedroom floor. As Barry entered the room, he was so accustomed to seeing me, himself, or other parents at the hospital sleeping anywhere in any position neither of us thought it strange that I was lying on the floor. He walked directly to his side of the bed, checked the alarm clock once more, and proceeded to lie down.

As I watched him, I was very much aware that I had slept throughout what should have been his time to sleep, for I had the "full night of sleep" taste in my mouth. Concerned that he would soon be going to work, I said nothing. Then finally I asked, "Is Steve OK? Is it morning?"

Groggily, Barry mumbled, "No, I just took over for you fifteen minutes ago. When I went to the room, he was half asleep; then he stopped tossing and turning, and fell into a deep sleep. You could not awaken him now if you tried."

God had answered my prayer! Not only had God put him to sleep, but He had also put me into the deepest sleep I have ever experienced. Those fifteen minutes of sleep were equal in effect to a whole eight hours of sleep. In fact, I was so completely rested and so filled with praise for what God had just done, I spent the remainder of the night praising Him.

Later, when I started to tell about some of these wonderful coincidences that could not come along by chance, I was reminded by my friend Susan that God's grace comes to His people in direct proportion to the enormity of the situation. I had asked her, "You know how He gives you peace when you should be hysterical?"

"No, I really don't, because I have never had a child that was ill unto death. God's grace matches the enormity of the problem."

God really did sit beside me as I sat beside the bed in the watches of the night.

***

Miracles of Relinquishment

Do not hold anything too tightly . . .

–Corrie Ten Boom

Abraham I was not. Certainly, I had not stood on Mount Moriah, raised the knife and trusted God to send a ram. Oh, I had had the wonderful experience of learning about God's love for me, but then there was that other voice I heard each morning when I read the newspaper and learned that yet another person had died of a type of childhood cancer. I was still afraid of the stalker–and he was a morning stalker, not a night one. How I could have allowed that morning voice to overrule the voice I had heard when I discovered God loved me, I do not know. Even four years after the diagnosis, I was still holding on tightly, not even letting God have a peek at this son with leukemia. He was clear of cancer now, by the grace of God. But I lived in constant fear that It would return. How soon I had suppressed those lessons I had learned from Dr. Peter Marshall about the love of God!

When God saw that I was weary of clutching tightly, when all of my resources finally ran dry, He met me, not on Mount Moriah, but on Black Mountain, in the foothills of the Great Smoky Mountains in North Carolina.

It was a Tuesday in July 1982. I was near Asheville, North Caroline, serving as sponsor at a large camp of eight hundred Fellowship of Christian Athlete Girls and hoping to enjoy a week of blessed rest and a renewal of my faith.

However, no sooner had I unpacked from the long bus ride from Indianapolis than the director of the camp, a former football player affectionately called Moose, announced that a very delicate situation would be dealt with on Tuesday evening. An eighteen-year-old Christian athlete, a cancer-stricken Bruce Banta from Atlanta, would be speaking to the girls. Heavily medicated, this very ill young fellow would tell the campers that life is short and ask them to evaluate how they are spending the time allotted to them. Because the girls would undoubtedly react by crying, probably uncontrollably, the staff of approximately thirty-five adults needed to be prepared to console eight hundred weeping girls.

My immediate reaction was fury. How could a God who loves me lead me into such a situation? After all, I had left a seventeen-year-old Christian athlete son at home who might also be dying with a cancer that was only in remission. Why did I have to have his future suffering portrayed for me? For instance, did I need details of how morphine is withheld in those last months so that its effectiveness wouldn't be depleted before the patient dies? I thought not.

Here I was, captive in a campground in the mountains–one road in–the same road out. The stalker had me cornered. This total isolation ensured that I had no choice but to deal with this situation. It was in this setting that God literally pried my tightly clutched fingers open and simply said, "Give me what is mine."

Anxious and fearful of what Bruce Banta would say, exhausted from years of rushing about telling people to give money to cancer research for children, and expending myself in any other activity that might help the situation, I mentally gave up the battle. Crumpled. Exhausted. Spent.

In moments after I had released what had been God's all along, I could see that all of this relinquishment had been part of a transaction between me and God. "You give to me what is mine, and I will generously give you a treasure." The moment I opened my clutched fist releasing to God what was His, God acknowledged that release as in an exchange. In the hours that followed, He began to share His secrets with me as He led me through the Bible, one passage after another, making personal applications. Even in my state of mind, I knew that such Bible studies with God as the leader were privileged times!

Let me describe my relinquishment scene in detail.

Only moments after Moose had prepared us for Bruce Banta's arrival, I separated myself from the other sponsors so I would be alone to think about this session. I ran to a chapel upstairs, a place built especially for the staff and special guests of this YMCA administration building. We campers were not using any of these facilities; therefore, I was certain I would be alone in here. it was very small, built to hold no more than ten people, with a piano at the short rows and sat silently for a moment. Afterall, I had no idea what to do; if I prayed, what would I pray?

Somehow it did not seem that I should pray that Bruce would not give his testimony. After some moments of silence, I began with a pleading prayer expressing my fears of losing my composure when the young man told his story. What purpose would I serve if I fell apart in front of eight hundred people? Then I asked, "Please God, you know how much words mean to me. would you favor me by showing a special Bible verse to strengthen me?" Fumbling, I took up the Bible and was almost afraid to open it. I took a deep breath and dumped all of the markers and camp registration papers out of my Bible. Then I opened it. Isaiah? What did Isaiah know about having a son with leukemia? Paul would have known about dealing with adversity, but Isaiah?

What did I have to lose? Cautiously, I looked down on words that took my breath away. In Isaiah 43:17, I began to read, . . . *extinguished, snuffed out like a wick; forget the former things; do not dwell on the past. See, I am doing a new thing! Now it springs up; do you not perceive it? I am making a way in the desert and streams in the wasteland.*

Only the person who lives with cancer in remission would get excited about such words as "extinguished, snuffed out, never to rise again." From the hour I read these words on that Tuesday afternoon in July 1982, I have believed that God was telling me to move on and forget about the leukemia. That chapter of our lives had been closed, the doctors and seemingly God now agreed that the cancer would not likely return as leukemia anyway, perhaps another type of cancer, but probably not as leukemia. There are no words to describe the ecstasy of that moment. My conservative request had been, "Lord, help me to endure the next three hours," past, present, and the future, words of blessed assurance that our son was really healed.

Wonderstruck, I moved out of that small, sun-filled chapel and climbed the hill to join the others to hear Bruce speak. As he spoke, I was wrapped in a strangeness that I cannot describe. What was happening around me was temporal, and where I was in those next two hours was eternal. Maybe I was where Bruce would soon be.

After Bruce had finished telling the girls how one by one he had lost limbs and opportunities to be in school and in sports, he was immediately escorted outside and injected with morphine to relieve the intense pain that, these days, never subsided. I moved quickly to touch him and to say, "Thank you."

Eager to be alone with "that verse" again, I slipped out of the sponsor's meeting and went to an isolated basement lounge area. What a wonderful night of reading and fellowship I had with the Lord, my rediscovered Friend. I asked questions, and He answered them immediately. Never before or since have I had such an experience with answered prayer.

First I asked, "What do you want me to do now?" I then read the Isaiah 43:17-21 passage again. There was the answer in the last verse: "that they may proclaim my praise." I was to tell others what God had done in my family, in my life.

I followed that answer with, "Do you want me to continue teaching in the high school?" He answered that by prompting me to scan the New Testament where I "arbitrarily" landed on Luke 24:49: "I am going to send you what my Father has promised; but stay in the city until you have been clothed with power from on high." I was to stay in the city, stay in my present teaching position.

While years later this encounter with God may seem unlikely to some, it was as real as if He had been seated beside me. What a relief to have additional affirmation after four years of no two-way conversation with Him beyond that serendipitous enlightenment about God's love for me, for all of us! It was chapter two in my own book of revelation!

Next I asked if this son should live; would his life be lived for God; would it be a life of worth or merely years that were squandered. In short, how could I rear him and his brother, who was deeply troubled by observing this strange illness in his older brother? For years these two sons had been alike, even were often dressed alike, played sports together, went everywhere together. Now for months Brian had been lonely and closely observant. Someone had told him that "leukemia can be fatal."

I returned to Isaiah 43:17-21 and read that again. My mind wandering, I simply glanced across the page and began to read in Isaiah 44:3, " . . . I will pour out my Spirit on your offspring, and my blessing on your descendants. They will spring up like grass in a meadow, like poplar trees by flowing streams. One will say, 'I belong to the Lord'; another will call himself by the name of Jacob; still another will write on his hand, 'The Lord's' and will take the name Israel.

At every question, I was given an immediate answer and a peace in my heart that I could never adequately describe today. I may never again have a night of such clear communication with God, but really, I don't need it. He answered questions in that one session that applied to my life from birth to eternal life.

In 1986, four years after this late-night reading and celebration, I had the opportunity to return to my Bethel–the place where I had met God face to face. Even though I was barely able to walk due to a back injury, I asked my husband to drive me out to that campground, for we were attending a conference in nearby Asheville. Barry parked the car, and I said I really wanted to go inside. I was glad he didn't want to accompany me because this was a personal mission. I dragged my body inside and went directly to the chapel. On this day it was an ordinary room, but that did not disappoint me. I knew that God had not stayed in that chapel all of those years, but instead He had walked with me and all of His other charges wherever we had gone. Satisfied, even with the ordinary room, I trudged back to the car. Even though my back muscles were really contracting, I smiled to myself recalling all of those mornings when we had been abruptly awakened by a loud blast from a tower higher up the mountain playing, "Nothing could be finer than to be in Carolina in the morning." Wondering if I would ever again return to this important meeting place in my Christian life, I looked back at my Bethel as we pulled away. I reasoned, "Yes, I will return to my Bethel every time God shares His secrets with me."

When I consider what I gathered from that experience, I could never imagine what Bruce Banta gained from sharing one of his last testimonies of how God was faithful to him even as he faced death.

Like a whirlwind's breath ...

His banner over me is love,
Our sword the Word of God;
We tread the road the saints above
With shouts of triumphs trod.

BY FAITH THEY LIKE A WHIRLWIND'S BREATH,

Swept on o'er every field
The faith by which they conquered death
Is still our shining shield.

In the interim years after the diagnosis of the leukemia, we dealt with the consequences of having a teen with cancer. We also tried to help a younger son deal with the reality of having a brother with what had been labeled potentially terminal.

There are individual ways of coping with "not being normal." Steve dealt with being different by trying to be like everyone else. Fortunately, his pranks and near misses remained just that–pranks and near misses. On the other hand, Brian, dealing with his own problems, some of which we knew nothing about, compensated for what he considered shortcomings and fears by being funny and generally avoiding anything academic.

From an objective approach, the doctors were quite amused and felt we should just "be there" and let these troubled youths, the patient and the sibling, work through their concerns in their own ways. Actually, the doctors agreed that both sons were reacting to living with serious childhood illnesses quite normally. Therefore, generally, we accepted their assessment and sighed with relief.

***

As we neared that hoped-for five-year milestone of Stephen being cancer-free, we had only occasional days when we doubted he would live. As always that nagging voice that interrupted our peace would be activated by a news report of someone else's death from Stephen's variety of leukemia. While on one level we had stopped lumping all cancers together as one disease and all leukemias as identical diseases, in our weak moments we would unwittingly heap all cancer into one big ugly bucket. On such days we would have to dredge up the events of that one day in August 1981 when Stephen went in for an evaluation that might end his protocol of chemotherapy several months early and he would possibly be declared disease-free, free as far as medical history could predict. We remembered the moment when Dr. Smith had announced:

"Steve appears to be one of those fortunate ones whose leukemia has remained in remission for twenty-two months. His condition has always remained stable. Therefore, we feel he probably will, barring no unforeseen interruptions, survive this disease for years to come."

His long remission and probable cure announcement came as a wonderful declaration. How can a person describe what it is like to run in front of a semi-truck for months on end, knowing that at any time she will be splattered onto the dead-end wall of the street? Then from the recesses of the mind hearing this wonderful news

"Don't worry. It seems that all of this has been nothing but a bad dream. You may start breathing deeply again."

Did I dare hold onto that protective part of me that wanted to prepare all of us for the way leukemia really ends? Or did I simply jump in with abandon and pull out all the stops and rejoice to the high heavens?!

It was true the biopsy and the blood counts had revealed no hidden cancer cells, and the doctor who wisely had withheld unsubstantiated hope until this moment had announced, "Shall we have a drum roll before I declare this disease is behind us?!

While we were leaping for joy, we were also in a fog. There had been a momentum we had maintained during the intense chemotherapy treatments, and now our emotions were grinding to an abrupt halt. Once we had enjoyed celebrating and a vacation from the "what if" syndrome, we found the adrenaline drained from your bodies.

I, for example, was exhausted. Yet my conversation with God at the Black Mountain Fellowship of Christian Athletes camp and the doctor's reports were believed. We could begin a new life! Our Stephen wasn't going to die just now! We were not going to die! That's right. I had always felt I was dying of cancer, too. Rarely do we meet a parent of a child with a serious illness who does not feel that way. I remembered the days in the springtime of the year when I had said as much on the subject: Barry was digging up some scraggy irises that were in bloom. I ran outside and yelled, "Don't dig up those irises. Don't you know I may never see irises again?!"

Now, all of that was a non-issue. Stephen was going to live. We were going to live to tell about a happy whiplash, a welcome "about face." What a truly wonderful boomerang—this change of events! Our family was home free!

Little did we know what loomed in our future . . .

***

Seven years later and in the year my grandmother died, our son Brian began to have mysterious spasms all over his body. In fact, three weeks before Grandmother's illness, Brian had become unusually nauseated and agitated during a family celebration. Having already walked quite a distance from the hotel where the reception had taken place, Brian announced to his brother and their friends that he needed to return to the reception to say "goodbye" to his great-grandmother. Since he had been ill most of the day and had been less than fun to be around, this latest complication was a real nuisance for them as they wanted to go on home.

Hurrying to reduce the amount of time he was taking, he went back inside and straight to his great-grandmother, who had always been a fan of Brian's, for she seemed to sense that he needed attention when most of the attention had been on his ill brother. As they stood together that day, I took a picture of them, a picture which has become very important to Brian.

He later told me that he felt more than a nudge to go back inside to say goodbye. Therefore, only a few days later when the diagnosis of Grandmother's illness was made, he knew what had moved him to return to bid her farewell. He never saw her again.

At grandmother's funeral only five weeks later, I noticed an unusual uneasiness in Brian, yet I understood that he was recalling God's hand on him that day of the reception. Indeed, Brian alone had been forewarned of what was to come. Also, since my grand-mother had been one of the most important people in my own life, I was fully immersed in my own loss and not really tuned to what Brian might have been thinking.

Two months later, Brian was hospitalized for "back problems" and was in traction for nine days. The orthopedic surgeon felt that traction would help Brian's back, yet at the same time, he was being diagnosed with fibromyalgia, inflammation of the muscles. So actually, the illness was a mystery. Finally, Brian dropped out of college, but we kept the apartment lease as assurance that he would soon be well enough to return.

In November of the same year, Brian spent eleven days in yet another hospital under the care of a "second opinion" neurologist secured by the orthopedic surgeon. His chronic back pain, diagnosed as caused by the herniated disc, had by now racked his body for six months, and his whole system was on the alert to subtle changes. Not knowing what was causing his problem, Brian was feeling very abnormal and had labeled himself a failure in school. Certainly, his college days were over. In short, he was losing out, falling behind, and maybe even dying of something no one was treating. Indicative of his low self-image and general devastation, he had set out for the hospital with two greeting cards previously sent to him on other occasions. One was a get-well card and one was an Easter card. When I discovered that he had brought those cards, especially the Easter card, I asked, "Why are you bringing the cards?" quite defensively, he answered, "I may not receive any cards this time. Everyone is tired of my illnesses.

In that very depressed state, Brian submitted to a battery of tests that were designed to point to a larger problem than that of the newly diagnosed slipped disc in his back. Meanwhile, we waited and actually expected the results to point to anxiety and depression, for by now, many of his family and friends had developed a somewhat condescending attitude toward Brian and his "hypochondria." Certainly, after Steve's leukemia, we thought Brian was thinking he, too, was very ill.

Then three days later, the news come. A spokesperson from a five-member neurosurgical team working on Brian's case was making his morning rounds when he dropped in and quite casually took a chair. Sitting at the foot of Brian's bed, he calmly said, "Brian has an impressively large tumor on the right frontal lobe of his brain."

Just like that. Almost eight years to the day that his older brother had heard the diagnosis of his leukemia, on this ordinary November Wednesday, Dr. C announced, "Brian has a brain tumor."

As many years of practice told me to choke on what I might have said, I responded in my most upbeat tone, "Brian can start working toward becoming completely well, now that we have the correct diagnosis."

Next, this doctor, who also could have been an academy award winner for his acting ability, said, "The tumor is changing and that fact has the neurosurgical team somewhat concerned," but he added they were preparing to "get this whipped soon. Just be patient with us, Brian." His words might have been soothing if I had not blurted out, "The tumor is changing?"

Dr. C knew I had really asked if Brian had a cancerous brain tumor. After all, I had another child at home with cancer in remission. Dr. C was well prepared for my reaction. "Oh, no, the tumor has been in place since birth or even before birth. The bone scan has revealed that the bones of Brian's skill are actually quite thin because the tumor has made its place inside the skull."

Temporarily, I was relieved that the tumor was not cancerous, but the lesser evil also opened another can of worms–what happened before birth was directly related to my role in Brian's prenatal development. "Was this a problem of genetics? An injury before birth? Some prescription drug I had taken while carrying him?"

No one could say.

A paper-thin skull to make way for a tumor?! How awful! Aghast at that thought, I mentally reviewed every contact sport, every car accident, every blow to his head that could have been disastrous. Dizzy from this review of each phase of the diagnostic announcement, I reminded myself that for Brian's sake I needed to project my "business as usual" composure. Quietly, I closed his drapes to darken the room and heeded his request that I leave so he could go to sleep. Down the hallway I flew without looking right or left. Once inside the elevator, I leaned against the wall. Exiting through the ground floor lobby, I broke into a run as I faced a gentle November rain and made my way through the long rows of cars in the parking lot. Freezing, trembling, crying, I jumped into the car and locked the doors . . . symbolically locking out everything, even brain tumors. "Not again" had me pinned to the wall.

Totally out of control, I pulled out of the parking lot intent on finding some place to hide and think through this most devastating news. Then I thought that maybe I could find a card or gift that I might use to distract Brian from this diagnosis. Brian loved cards. I would find him a card. Shocked, exhausted and heartsick, I really didn't know what to do. In this state of mind, I prayed in not such a prayerful tone:

"God, I've already done this. You know I have. What kind of a trick is this? I have done everything you wanted. This is your reward? If you want to talk to me about something, why not talk directly to me and leave my sons alone."

Sobbing and driving through the gray drizzle, I quieted myself after my sharp-tongued conversation with God, then began to pray in a more humble tone, yet I was still having trouble forgetting that I really had already "given at the office." One son, but not two, Lord.

Brian and Great-grandmother, Lois Leonard, on May 30, 1986. She passed on in July and Brian was diagnosed with brain tumor in November.

Brian three weeks two days after brain surgery in October 1987.

God, you know I am alone today. His dad has to go to work sometime to pay these bills. Besides, how can I call him and tell him this terrible news over the phone? I am Brian's only source of strength this afternoon. He needs answers, for after all, he, too, has done this before with his brother, Steve. I cannot help him because you have given me nothing to cling to except the old saying, 'You did it before, you can do it again.' But you and I know that I am eight years older, and the fact is, I cannot go through "it" again.

In a strip mall parking lot, encased in a car pelted with heavy rain, I picked up my Bible and half-heartedly opened it. Since Psalm 139 is a favorite of mine, the spine of the Bible opens to it easily; therefore, today, the Bible fell open at Psalm 139. This chapter has blessed me many, many times, but today I was less than happy, knowing there is nothing about brain tumors in Psalm 139. Wouldn't one think that at least God would lead me to a hopeful passage that directly applied to our situation? Convinced that God was not in the tune with my problem, I decided to read the favorite Psalm anyway. What else did I have to consult?

Starting where my eyes fell, I began with verse 14, which reads:

I praise you because I am fearfully and wonderfully made, your works are wonderful, I know that full well. My frame was not hidden from you when I was made in the secret place. When I was woven together in the depths of the earth, your eyes saw my unformed body. All the days ordained for me were written in your book before one of them came to be.

(NIV)

I stopped in total disbelief. God was there in the car beside me. He knew I was desperate. He was going to help us deal with this brain tumor!

I drove the few blocks to a drugstore and found a card that would replace the Easter card on the night stand. Without hesitation, I wrote this Psalm 139: 14-16 passage in the card. I then decided I would hurry back to the hospital to give the card to Brian and tell him the good news.

Intent on returning, I turned the ignition key, and the local Christian radio station came on. Fortunately, I did not turn it off, but rather listened to one of the sweetest songs I have ever heard. David Meese was singing "Wonderfully Made." It was as though God, wanting to punctuate what he had already said in Psalm 139, enlisted David Meese to sing the Words of the Bible to me. He must have thought I might forget.

***

Christmas 1987

One month after the diagnosis of Brian's brain tumor, we attended Christmas Eve services at church. Pastor David Powell, our minister at that time, read from Luke 1:26-56. The passage begins with "Greetings, you are highly favored! The Lord is with you. Mary was greatly troubled . . ." then the passage ends with Mary's song of joy.

Very receptive, hanging on to every word, I heard "highly favored," "greatly troubled" and "song of joy" conflicting yet used together. I knew there was a message for me on this Christmas with one son's leukemia in remission and one son's brain tumor under observation "to see if it changes." On the one hand, I had the wonderful joy of Christmas and all that goes with Christmas, and on the other hand I was terrified.

What a relief to know that seemingly paradoxical emotions of fear and joy can reside side by side in a person committed to God. Also, as in Mary's life, joy will eventually win!

Anyone who lives with a chronic illness or a potentially terminal illness will agree that the most difficult days are those in which the most wonderful and the most feared take up residence in the same mind. Praise be to God that Mary's song of joy resolves that dilemma for all of us! Of course she was afraid, yet she had joy in her heart.

Soon Christmas had passed and my thoughts were returning to "that impressively large tumor." In fact, for the next seven months, my thoughts rarely strayed from thinking about it, constantly analyzing events nineteen years earlier to discover its source.

In July, Brian's back problems escalated, and a myelogram test was ordered. This test, one which most patients dread, involves injecting dye into the spine. Unknown to the doctors or to us, the dye appeared to awaken the "sleeping lion," and what had been described as benign, began to yawn and press the brain stem.

Two weeks later, the night before the disc surgery, Brian told us that something was very wrong. If he stared at stationary objects, they eventually moved. Very concerned but realizing the night-before-the-surgery-jitters were common, we dismissed his announcement that something far greater than a herniated disc was really the diagnosis. "Obviously, any nineteen-year-old would fear major surgery," we reasoned.

The following day the surgery proceeded as planned. This major procedure of fusing ruptured discs of the spinal column is delicate and postponed by people twice the age of Brian, and yet in his situation, the surgery was minor compared to other future surgeries and future treatments of his experience. Little did we know what lay ahead.

In short, the microscopic incision in the back healed well. Only a week later, Brian began to notice that stationary objects moved or blurred even more than they had before the surgery. Clearly, the brain tumor had not gone away. Fortunately, we did not know the seriousness of Brian's condition. Yet the doctor was keenly aware of what was happening. Even though Brian was young and would heal easily, having another major surgery so soon after the surgery on his back, would create a major loss of blood, not to mention great stress to his system.

Numerous tests were performed; the neurosurgeons evaluated the results. Again, quietly, the doctors took a "wait and see" approach. Even though to us Brian's condition appeared to be very unstable, the surgeons pressed for at least six weeks of recuperation from the disc surgery before operating on what was an inoperable brain tumor. At best, they would insert a shunt to relieve pressure to the "distressed" brain stem.

Meanwhile, as if this change in Brian's health coupled with the remission of cancer in the other son were not enough, my husband was hearing rumors at work that his company was downsizing. For seventeen years when Stephen was well, we had truly planned our calendar around the business and social events of this company. Often when his work took him all over the country, I had traveled with him. How could it be that he would not have this job? Only days earlier, when Brian had undergone his back surgery, the company had sent two large bouquets of flowers and balloons and "Best Wishes." This company was part of our family.

Realizing that the job seemed threatened, I suggested that my husband make clear to the owners that we were waiting for Brian's body to heal somewhat in order for him to undergo the dreaded brain surgery. Certainly, I reasoned, once they knew our circumstances, they would move my husband somewhere else in the company.

This was not to be. The plan was clear: One by one, the vice presidents were losing their jobs, and this month my husband had been selected to start the process of downsizing.

The job had been terminated. The message: *In 30 days Barry will be let go. He should apply for a new job as soon as possible, but of course, in the next four months, he will have full salary severance pay.*

And so, on my forty-fifth birthday, my husband's car pulled down the lane to our house filled with all of the personal effects of seventeen years of working. Labor Day festivities also began on this day, not to mention that the seriousness of son Brian's condition was escalating daily. In fact, shortly after this day, the brain tumor that had been relatively dormant for almost nineteen years presented its true personality.

Meanwhile, in order to keep our sanity, we took long walks in the evenings. We walked for exercise, but also to have a chance to get an update on the job prospects and the new symptoms of Brian's tumor–all of which we did not want Brian to hear. Thus, the walking gave us privacy to plan our method of approach to our many problems.

One particular evening when we were into our second lap of the nightly walk on the street that circled our neighborhood, Brian, back at our house, fell face forward as he reached the landing of the stairway to go upstairs. For seconds he could not move, but then he dragged himself across the stairway landing and yelled to us. We couldn't hear–we were out walking! Unaware of his calling to us, we walked on.

Brian then dragged himself to the phone and made arrangements for his admission into the emergency ward of a city hospital. When we arrived a few minutes later, he was ready to leave for the hospital.

In a highly practiced rush, we knew how to mobilize immediately. We knew to grab the grocery bag and line it with a tall kitchen plastic bag, then roll the tops together. This was for the possible upset stomach. We had done this scores of times in the past eight years. Also, we knew which type of car-seat-reclining-position was appropriate for which type of illness. Each time we burst through the door of the emergency room, we carried what we needed, much as our friends carried what they needed for a weekend on their boat. Over those years of emergency runs, we had learned to view these quick turns as business as usual. However, the following day, we were to learn that this particular trip was far from usual.

Around midnight, once the neurosurgeon had checked out the situation, nineteen-year-old Brian was admitted to the hospital for observation. Not knowing the seriousness of this new development and by now being practical even in emergencies, Barry and I went home to rest, for we suspected that the following day's medical test results would inevitably be negative. We also needed to make arrangements with our work places and to get some sleep in order to be strong in case of new developments in Brian arose. This complete confidence that he was resting well without our presence was very unusual in our family, for usually we were somewhere in the hospital when a seriously ill son was being treated. Early the following morning, Brian called. Emergency surgery had been scheduled for 2:00 pm that same day!

Once I had canceled the college classes I was teaching that day, I hurried to the hospital to be with him. Very agitated and by then wanting to delay the surgery, he said he didn't think he was mentally prepared for it. Of course, we told him we would have to talk with his doctor. I marvel now that we were totally unaware of the seriousness of the situation. Yet I don't know why I am surprised, for the same cushioning had been going on for years. God, building on the lessons he had taught heretofore, was holding us in his comforting arms.

Finally, at Brian's insistence, I called the surgical suite to speak with the neurosurgeon who was busy making the transition between surgeries. I told him Brian had asked if the surgery might be delayed. With little time for elaboration, he minced no words by saying that Brian's left side was already showing signs of paralysis, and if he were left unattended, he would soon become totally paralyzed on the left side and/or would die. Furthermore, he said, Brian should be expecting a gurney to come for him soon.

Zombie-like, I quietly replaced the receiver. Telling only what was necessary to Brian, I steeled myself for the next few moments of gently leading him into the next few hours. We exchanged final goodbyes. This was the second time, the second son with whom I had said a final goodbye.

Soon after, the orderly came with the gurney to whisk Brian away to the surgical corridor where he would be alone for the next few minutes. MY SON–I was a helpless mother waiting for Brian to undergo something neither his father nor I had faced in our own lives. Such is the feeling of parents of children with serious illnesses. I was ashamed to expect him to do what I had never done myself.

The following Christmas poem-story, written a few weeks later and set in September, best describes what happened in the twenty-four hours that followed our final farewell before the surgery:

A Christmas story
(Set in September)

I became the curve in the u-shaped setting,
For unfolding out from me on both sides
Were overlapping newspapers
Turned to the same page
Behind each newspaper, a reader
Read intently–
Oblivious to my presence,
Thankful for the newspaper,
An acceptable diversion.
Yes, all of us
Waited for the results of someone's surgery,
But only my loved one's surgery
And that news story were related.
For an instant, every reader held the
Newspaper turned to
The caricature of an ailing hospital,
A thermometer protruding out its front door.
A medical company in difficult times
Protesting to the media,
"We have had to release only ONE employee to date."
Presently that employee, my husband,
Had his back to me

Just beyond the newspaper overlap,
I could see him in the hallway.
Looking tired,
He leaned on the door frame
Of a public phone booth.
A poignant moment–
For behind closed doors, doctors
Performed emergency brain surgery
To prevent a son's threatening paralysis;
While outside in the hallway,
A weary, middle-aged father
Dropped money into a public phone
To ask for a job–any job.
And I,
Continuing my vigil as part of the newspaper collage,
Watched, as suddenly the news pages turned.
Like the changing design in a kaleidoscope
And rightly so, my perspective had changed also,
For through the waiting room door
Burst our older son whose own ill health
Had many times brought me to my knees.
Today a college speech had prompted him
To wear coat and tie–
This scrubbed appearance,
A mother's fantasy became reality,
Caught me off guard.
In my lapse of recognition
A bit of truth was revealed–
For when a child is seriously ill,
All of that mother's children are
Toddlers again–
Momentarily, I did not know this young man,
Who should have been dressed in faded denim,
Who should have been much younger.
Then it happened–
As my husband and son joined me,
The kaleidoscopic picture in my mind

Swirled out of pattern, out of focus,
Into a new design—
For there we sat
Waiting for the results of one son's
Emergency brain surgery!
My newly defrocked vice president husband
On one side
My older son with leukemia in remission,
On the other side.
Ah! A catch in my whole body—
Surely nothing in the remaining years
Of my life
Would produce a set of circumstances
More poignant
Than those of this moment!
Hours later,
In a medically supervised room upstairs,
Our son and I settled in for the night.
"There will be seizures, some violent,"
The doctor had warned.
But now, our boy slept,
Fitfully,
Yet he slept.
Exhausted, but alert,
I turned from the bed
To the window
As in every trying time of my life,
I had always run to the window
In hopes of seeing some escape perhaps.
Serving as a welcome entertainment,
The heliport pad on the opposite wing,
One-half story above our room,
Quivered with activity.
With colored lights outlining the launch site
On this crisp, clear September night,
A helicopter, emptied of its patient,
Prepared for another emergency run.

Intently watching the activity
Of someone else's trauma
I felt a change develop
Before my eyes,
On the most devastating, emergency-filled day,
The beacon tower above the launch pad
Shot out a blinding light—
A shaft of light sufficient to blind me
And under this shaft of light,
The lower lights began to twitch and turn.
Suddenly,
This light show
Bathed my
Aching life
With a hope born at Christmas.
As the helicopter lights
Blended with
The beam of light
That played
On the lower colored lights,
Showers of platinum and crystal
Danced in the air.
In that blinding beacon
I saw God's love
Interacting with my broken dreams
And those of other families here nearby me.
Our various personas
In our various heritages
And in our various dilemmas.
Then sweetly the words of Christmas hope played on my mind.
It came upon the midnight clear,
That glorious song of old,
From angels bending near the earth
To touch their harps of gold.
Peace on the earth,
Goodwill to men,
From heaven's all gracious king:

The world in solemn stillness lay
To hear the angels sing.
And ye beneath life's crushing load,
Whose forms are bending low,
Who toil along the climbing way
With painful steps and slow,
Look now! For glad and golden hours
Come swiftly on the wing:
O rest beside the weary road
And hear the angels sing.

The warm September air–
Now electric with moanings
From the slumbering, suffering one beside me
Was then filled with the sweetest song of all–
The benediction to all suffering ...
... Be near me, Lord Jesus!
I ask thee to stay
Close by me forever,
And love me I pray.
Bless all the dear children
In Thy tender care,
And fit us for heaven,
To live with thee there.
Throughout the night watch, as I waited for the seizures
Forecast in the prognosis, the words sang:
The world in solemn stillness lay
To hear the angels sing.

Slowly, Brian recovered. Throughout the autumn months, every nerve in his body adjusted, as the shunted, inoperable tumor shrank. Also, one by one, a variety of specialists helped Brian live with the unusual symptoms that accompanied this adjustment to the straightening brain stem. First the ailment had been infection in his muscles, next the herniated disc, then there was the brain tumor, and now, after the surgery the problem seemed to be with the kidneys and colon. Plus elevators or any change of altitude left him clutching the walls to regain his balance. We knew what was happening; as the brain stem was straightening, the whole body was adjusting. Yet this convalescence was frustrating to a nineteen year old.

In October, he took pictures of all the extraordinarily beautiful autumn leaves. All around the restored canning factory office building where Barry now worked were stately old maples with old-gold-colored leaves. The contrast of those colors against the very old brick and wooden factory was breathtaking. We concluded that somehow Brian's picture-taking, the challenge of getting just the right shot, the right angle, the right light, was wonderfully therapeutic.

Finally, three months after the surgery, we decided that maybe he needed a change of scenery. We all did. We rented a van and drove to the Peach Bowl Football Game in Atlanta. Here we saw he was having trouble getting off the escalators in Peachtree Center. He descended in a disoriented and panicky state. The change of altitude disturbed him more than any other situation. All in all, after months of unpredictable recovery, we now concluded that relieving pressure on the brain stem is a very delicate, risky, yet life-saving business.

By March, after the September surgery, Brian was able to return to college and enroll in one class in world history in the spring quarter. In a small but significant victory, he proved one of the neurologists wrong by making a "B" in this normally dreaded, three-hour class.

Only three months after the Atlanta trip, we felt certain that Brian would benefit from another trip away from parents, the trusted neurosurgeon, and the close proximity of the familiar hospital. We encouraged him to go on a spring break trip with some close friends five months after his surgery for the shunted brain tumor. Even though he was going to Ft. Lauderdale, reportedly a spring break place where few people eat right or get plenty of sleep, we reasoned that after all, he and his friends were now older and wiser. The driver was the one who had visited Brian in the hospital; also, the other friends knew about the problems of adjustment he had been encountering while convalescing. They had seen him when he was dizzy after riding in an elevator, when he became tired and required rest, yet those observations had not discouraged them. They wanted him to go with them.

Three nights into the trip, our phone rang at 11:00 pm. Brian was calling from the emergency room of a hospital in Ft. Lauderdale.

"Oh?" was my standard reply to such unexpected phone calls. Then after the usual response, I blurted out, "Brian, are you all right? What has happened?"

By now Barry was on the extension phone as Brian began to tell us about the numbness all down his left side. I diagnosed as he spoke. "He's having a stroke," was the repeated recording in my brain.

Trying not to sound alarmed, we gave the insurance numbers so the non-English-speaking hospital staff could examine him. Our final words were, "Call when you return to your motel room. We will not go to sleep until we hear from you."

Thinking ahead even as we said our goodbyes, I was mentally making airplane reservations, when I remembered that a major airline was on strike. Few could obtain a ticket to Ft. Lauderdale over spring break even in the best of times.

As I thumbed through the phone book, I halfheartedly prayed. The only audible part of that prayer was a one-liner, "Lord, send him a companion, a friend who knows the way." Then as I frantically continued to make a plane reservation, I thought to myself, "What a dumb prayer! My son is having a stroke, and I am praying that he have a companion, a friend!"

Telling myself he was surely becoming paralyzed on the left side, I ripped through the phone book and called every airline company listed on the page. Finally I relayed our problem to an agent who earnestly began to search for a spare ticket to Ft. Lauderdale. In a few minutes she had located a one-way ticket out of Cincinnati leaving the following morning at 7:30 AM.

Barry and I discussed the plan for him to drive to Cincinnati, take the one-way ticket to Ft. Lauderdale, and then rent a car to bring Brian home. Our plans were set by the time the phone rang again around 1:00 AM. With me hovering near the phone, Barry took the call.

Immediately, I could detect a new tone in their conversation. They were discussing the problems of communication with people who did not speak English. What kind of a conversation was this? Here he was having a stroke, and they were discussing culture shock!

Very soon Brian told his dad he didn't want anyone to fly down. He said he felt very tired and simply needed a good night's rest to let the medication do the work. Then he said, "I need to talk to Mom."

Certain that I could persuade him to come home, I took the phone. I could hardly believe the change in his voice from that earlier conversation.

"Mom, you know how you and I have talked about coincidences that happen, weird stuff–you will not believe what happened to me tonight. I was leaving the hospital with my medication, feeling more upset, more tired and more sick than I have ever felt. Everyone around me was Spanish-speaking, and my friends, not knowing how sick I was, were spending the night in Key West. I felt very much alone. Almost everyone here in the waiting room tonight had overdosed on something; most emergency room patients were filthy. What a depressing place!

"I called a taxi and waited. By the time I had stepped into the cab, I was ready to break down. I never felt so alone, when the cab driver turned to ask me where I was going, I could not believe that yet another person spoke in Spanish. I guess I must have looked as bad as I felt because without hesitation the cab driver turned back around and picked up a card from the front seat, then reached back to give me the card. In my weary state, I do not even know why I looked down at it. I guess I wanted to see what Spanish looks like. You will not believe what that card said in English:

Let not your heart be troubled;
Ye believe in God,
Believe also in me.
In my Father's house
Are many mansions:
If it were not so,
I would have told you.
And if I go and prepare a place
For you, I will come again,
And receive you unto myself;
That where I am, there ye may be also.

John 14: 1-3–KJV

"Mom, I know you have said things like that have happened to you, but that was too-o-o-o weird. Where did that taxi driver come from? I do know he was in the right place at the right time. Well, I am exhausted. I know I will feel better tomorrow."

Ecstatic, I put the receiver down. I recalled my mumbled, one-line prayer, "Lord, please send him a companion, a friend who knows the way." (Or had I said THE WAY?) I had prayed but had not really expected to receive an answer. Certainly I had no idea that God, who was hearing my prayer as it floated through the heavens above Indianapolis, could act on the object of that prayer in Ft. Lauderdale, Florida!

The results of prayer exceed what we mortals could have done. It was far better that I pray in Indiana than that I sit in the hospital waiting room in Ft. Lauderdale. My presence and care would be minimal compared to what God could do with a prayer from Indiana or anywhere!

As I put down the receiver of the phone that night, I remembered a discussion I had heard that had undoubtedly influenced my conclusion on this late night vigil.

A few months earlier, we were seated at a church carry-in dinner. Several women were talking about how they worry when their sons and daughters are out at night. Fortunately for us, Tom Walker joined the group. When he could no longer tolerate what he was hearing, he calmly, but firmly said, "It constantly amazes me that you mothers believe you can protect your child better than God can."

Tom was right. Why would anyone assume the power of greater protection than God can provide?

***

By the time of the Ft. Lauderdale experience. I had come to value my time in an organized Bible Study. I had discovered a wonderful pleasure in marking passages that especially blessed me on specific occasions. Yes, I even took the time to write the date in the margin of my Bible. Well documented are those occasions, and also included are the names of those people who led me in finding those particular passages.

Valuable tools in building my faith, these passages proved to me that God had been "there" on other occasions; therefore, I could know that he would be faithful in present and future times as well.

Today, in light of twenty years of dealing with the illnesses in our sons, I should not be surprised to find that the margin beside Psalm 63 is loaded with one date after another in remembrance of those times when God and I stood guard during a night watch!

Also the beloved Psalm 23 is well marked. In my study of that passage, someone led me to ask myself, "What table is God preparing before me?" that question has been a valuable tool for me to use in analyzing "What's happening now?" Always after I have spent time with that question, I conclude that the entrée God prepares is palatable when viewed from His eternal perspective.

I know that eleven years of well-planned, well-prayed-over Bible studies gave me the daily tools with which to deal with the illnesses of our sons. No matter what the passage chosen for the week, it always fit my circumstances right then. Amazing! For instance, I could even see in the story of David running form King Saul strength for standing by as, over a period of years, our sons underwent numerous tests. God was with David in that thirteen-year trial, and He would be with us in our trial of as many years and more. I could also see that one day that trial would be over, and that day could be today!

I could see my desire for a quick fix to end all our sons' suffering in the story of Jehosaphat and King Ahab. In the course of events, Jehosaphat finally compromises and joins the ranks of the evil King Ahab. How often did I want to compromise and do anything–good or evil–to end or relieve suffering.

All in all, I know the Bible study fit into my life at exactly the time God had prescribed. Never again will I assume that Isaiah knew nothing about dealing with leukemia nor that there is nothing about dealing with a brain tumor in Psalm 139! Also, never again will I assume that I can live a fulfilled life without including a daily study of the Bible.

In fact, in those eleven years of organized weekly Bible study, I discovered two Bible stories, favorite passages that have spoken to me over and over again. They are the stories of Noah and of Nehemiah, both found in the Old Testament and both so thoroughly modern I could assume they were written only yesterday. I have reached certain personal applications from both of these powerful stories.

No doubt, a complete understanding of the story of Noah's Ark is sufficient to cover the message of the entire Bible. Certainly in the story of Noah there is the story of creation and the story of the judgment day–Genesis to Revelation in one story.

In fact, as I sit at the computer right now, I am looking at a large wooden ark on the chest on the opposite wall of my office. For me, it is the symbol of the security I have in Jesus Christ, the ultimate Ark of Safety.

Noah was blameless among his peers, yet all others, except his family, were corrupt. One day as Noah was walking with God in his prayers and devotion, God told him, "Noah, build an ark." Then God told him that He would destroy the earth and all the creatures of the earth. He made a covenant with Noah, telling him that he and his wife, sons, and their wives should enter the Ark and be safe. Noah was to take a male and female of each species of animals and place them inside the Ark also. Then God would close the door from the outside.

And so these things came to pass.

Then It rained for forty days and forty nights. After a dove returned to Noah carrying an olive branch, Noah knew the flood was over and the water was receding.

Why does this story thrill me so?

Noah's safe haven was an ark. My ark is the arms of Jesus, who paid the price for my sins. In my ark of safety, the arms of Jesus, I have a peace that lasts forever. As I float over the difficult floodwaters of life, I am secure in my ark of safety. I am totally at peace.

Nehemiah speaks to me, too. He speaks to all who have medical, financial, or other types of problems, for he had a crisis on his hands. Nehemiah had heard that the walls of Jerusalem were broken down. In ancient cities, the wall provided the fortress; therefore, a broken wall was unsafe; it was disgraceful for the walls of a city to be in ruins. While there is much to say about this city and this builder, the part that speaks to me and to anyone who has suffered would surely be the discussion of the inspection of the wall by night (Nehemiah 2:11-18).

Night. Illness knows no rest, no respite. Fevers escalate at night. Reactions from chemotherapy and radiation reach their peak during the night after the day's treatment. Fear of the prognosis reaches its height at night. As I related earlier, so prevalent have night and the events of night been in our household I have prepared myself by meditating on Psalm 63:6-8

On my bed I remember you;
I think of you through the watches of the night.
Because you are my help,
I sing in the shadow of your wings.
My soul clings to you;
Your right hand upholds me.

I have also prepared for nighttime in practical ways. Years after the need for preparation has ended, I continue to prepare. I suspect that all parents of children with serios illnesses will forever be alert. For instance, my shoes and clothes are assembled near the bed. Our car has enough gasoline to go twenty-two miles . . . to the emergency room. I continue to keep adjusting my days and nights to conform to what others call day and night. I can sleep on any floor, or spend the night leaning on any wall. I know no home base at nighttime. Any room can be called a bedroom.

Night. I know what it means to be a part of the night watch; therefore, I can see Nehemiah as he secretly surveys the damage to the walls of Jerusalem. Every parent of a child with a serious illness has ridden along with Nehemiah, mentally assessing the diagnosis and prognosis and all in between.

He begins:

I set out during the night with a few men. I had not told anyone what my God had put in my heart to do for Jerusalem. There were no mounts with me except the one I was riding on (vs. 11-12).

Alone!

Having quieted the family for the night, the vigilant one quietly searches the ceiling as though she were searching for answers.

Quietly, the mind rides on, first passing the Valley Gate, then going through the Dung Gate, next riding through the Fountain Gate, then following the narrow path around the king's pool, on and on, going up the valley by night surveying the damage.

Finally, that weary vigilant one returns to the Valley Gate and says:

"You see the trouble we are in. We lie in ruins. Come let us rebuild."

***

Along about the time that I could see my own situation in the stories of Noah and Nehemiah, Dr. Charles Lake of Greenwood, Indiana, introduced me to the wonderful concept of abiding with Jesus. As Dr. Lake built the foundation for the principle of abiding, I recalled that Grandmother had played "Beyond the Sunset," "Ivory Palaces," and always "Abide with Me" for every funeral I had ever attended before I went to college. Therefore, I naturally concluded that "Abide with Me" was reserved as a funeral song. I learned a most valuable lesson about abiding from Dr. Charles Lake. As he spoke about vines attached to stems, I remembered the garden we had planted each year when I was growing up.

Yes, as Dr. Charles Lake spoke I thought about those gardens that had produced rhubarb, dill, pumpkins, peanuts, sweet potatoes, parsnips, turnips, gooseberries, as well as all of the more normally expected Hoosier garden-fare.

"Abide is a favorite word of mine and introduces a wonderful concept," Dr. Lake continued.

I am the vine; you are branches. If a man remains in me and in him, he will bear much fruit; apart from me you can do nothing . . . if you remain in me and my words remain in you, ask whatever you wish, and it will be given to you . . .

John 15:5,7 NIV.

Then my mind wandered back to those watermelons and pumpkins that lolled around all day long attached to the vines that curled around them and shaded them.

Pastor Lake closed by portraying the source of our nourishment and God's provision for us: "Day after day, year after year, all we have to do is remain attached to the vine."

I saw myself abiding, making sure nothing severed my ties from the vine. Resting in the cool shade of my leafy sanctuary, I reasoned that I could be renewed every day and never wilt

Then I realized I had been abiding for twenty years and had mistakenly thought that abiding was reserved for those facing death. Abiding is about living!

"What a wonderful concept comes from that word, ABIDE!" Dr. Lake concluded.

When my sister Karen played the church's piano and I played the organ, we chose our own songs–a privilege that benefits those who can play only those songs with one sharp or one flat! Often we played "Faith Is the Victory" because the difficulty of deciphering the music was less than that of other hymns. The truth comes out when I admit that I really thought the long "Faith Is the Victory" produced a monotony that is difficult for even the greatest song leader to overcome. Therefore, I was quite surprised when I really listened to the lyrics of the fifth line of the second verse of none other than the droning "Faith Is the Victory." Here it was twenty years after we had played it at church, as children inheriting Grandmother's job as pianist:

His banner over me is love,
Our sword the Word of God;
We tread the road the saints above
With shouts of triumphs trod.
By faith they like a whirlwind's breath,
Swept on o'er every field
The faith by which they conquered death
Is still our shining shield.

Spinning, spinning with a wide vortex and then a narrow vortex, the breath of my faith had spun through much trouble, but now I could change that final verse of my poem about such spinning:

A WHIRLWIND'S BREATH

Karen saw it coming
Down by the garden
Whirling among the orchard's
Pear trees.
At first it spun low to the ground,
But by the time it reached
The big oak that Grandma
Had grazed on her first and final
Driving lesson,
It had picked up enough dust
To spread wide and accelerate
Full speed ahead.

From our perch on the porch swing,
We watched intently as it followed
The road, passing the apple trees
And heading straight for the lilac bush.
A top spinning with more determination
Than I had ever witnessed,
It wheeled around the lilac
And the top of the well, skipped the coal pile,
Ducked under the lowest limbs
Of the tulip tree,
And executed a flourish,
As if to wave to the viewers
On the porch swing.
Then it whistled by the hop vine
That Grandma had tied with twine
To the corner post of the porch,

And smooth as my Daddy's whistle,
It spun completely out of sight.

Amazed, we children sat quietly
For a few moments,
Reviewing what we had seen
And listening for a crash
Somewhere in the backyard
As the whirlwind would surely
Collide with something in its path.

Not moving a muscle,
We waited,
We listened.

Once we had felt the
Warmth of the whirlwind's breath,
We never forgot how powerfully
That swish sailed by.

Decades later,
We wait,
We listen.

Then we settle back
In his love.

Epilogue

I count the colors of the leaves at the edge of Indiana's Road 37—plum, celery, old gold, to name a few. I recall days of mushroom picking in the springtime and hickory nut gathering in the fall. I am certain that it was in the rich folds in the hills of Southern Indiana that I learned valuable coping skills to deal with the years that I have described in this book. Whatever it was, we harvested it, preserved it. Whatever hardship, we met it head-on.

This past year, we buried both of Barry's parents who had taught us how to do what we had to do. over and over, I see that my mother, Eunice McCart, who was mourning the loss of my father during much of the time Stephen and Brian were ill, prepared me to be strong and able in all circumstances.

Those childhood years were strengthening years, yet I attribute my peace to God, the Enabler. It was the Enabler who made me whole when I was weak, who went before all of us and carried us along.

Today, decades after Brian's illness, we rejoice in the health of our two sons whose story I have told. Steve, husband of Kim, father of Brittany and Allison, enjoys good health with the occasional residual effects of having had chemotherapy. He is CEO of Healthcare Therapy Services.

...he suffers few consequences from that treatment nor do his children.

Brian, husband of Donna and father of Abigail, Emily, and Carter has no complications from his early illness and enjoys work as Corporate Recruiter for Healthcare Therapy Services.

–Judith McCart Chatham
Summer 2024

The author can be contacted via:

Author's Tranquility Press
3900 N Commerce Dr. Suite 300 #1255
Atlanta, GA 30344
www.authorstranquilitypress.com

Brian and Steve at Ball State University, August 1989.

Brian at age 17 in June 1994.

Steve, Susan, Allison and Brittany, "Life is good!"

Donna, Brian and Abigail Elizabeth on Christening Day,
March 1, 1998.

At Bonds Chapel in Hindostan today. Gian picnic tables face the cemetery. A few miles down the road is the original Hindostan Falls, wiped out by a yellow fever epidemic, leaving it as Indiana's most significant ghost town.

The Orangeville General Store has operated on this site for nearly a hundred years. Its rustic practicality is typical of my home county–then and now!

Riley Hospital today–the old landmark covered by a new pavilion.

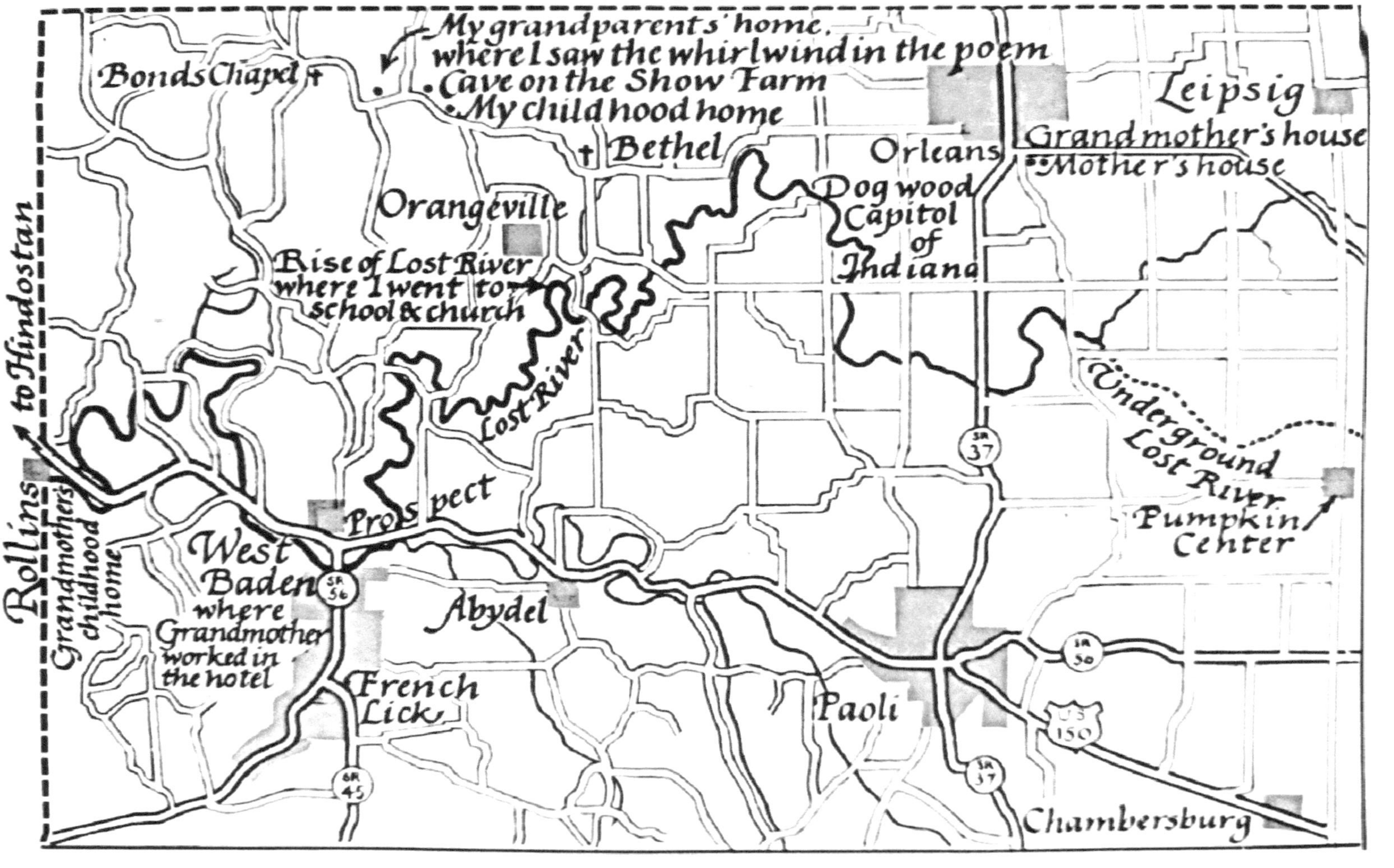

My grandparents' home, where I saw the whirlwind in the poem
Cave on the Show Farm
My childhood home
Bonds Chapel
Leipsig
Grandmother's house
Mother's house
Orleans
Bethel
Dogwood Capitol of Indiana
Orangeville
Rise of Lost River where I went to school & church
Lost River
Underground Lost River
SR 37
Pumpkin Center
Prospect
West Baden where Grandmother worked in the hotel
SR 56
Abydel
Rollins to Hindostan
Grandmother's childhood home
French Lick
SR 45
Paoli
SR 50
US 150
SR 37
Chambersburg